NUTS

C000204114

COMMERCIAL LAW
IN A
NUTSHELL

AUSTRALIA
Law Book Company
Sydney

CANADA and USA
Carswell
Toronto

HONG KONG
Sweet & Maxwell Asia

NEW ZEALAND
Brookers
Wellington

SINGAPORE and MALAYSIA
Sweet & Maxwell Asia
Singapore and Kuala Lumpur

NUTSHELLS

COMMERCIAL LAW IN A NUTSHELL

FIRST EDITION

by

EWAN MACINTYRE,
School of Law,
Nottingham Trent University

London • Sweet & Maxwell • 2006

*Published in 2006 by Sweet & Maxwell Limited of
100 Avenue Road, London, NW3 3PF
Typeset by LBJ Typesetting Ltd of Kingsclere
Printed in The Netherlands by Krips of Meppel*

No natural forests were destroyed to make this product.
Only farmed timber was used and re-planted.

A CIP catalogue record for this book is available
from the British Library.

ISBN 0 421 797 401
9780421797406

©
Sweet & Maxwell
2006

CONTENTS

1. DEFINITIONS WITHIN THE SALE OF GOODS ACT 1979

Section 1(1) of the Sale of Goods Act 1979 (the SGA) tells us that the Act applies to contracts of sale of goods. So if a contract does not fit within the definition of a contract of sale of goods then the Act will not apply to it.

Contract of sale of goods

Section 2(2) defines a contract of sale of goods as a contract by which the seller transfers or agrees to transfer the property in goods to the buyer for a money consideration called the price. In order to understand what is meant by this we need to know the meaning of several things: a contract; goods; the property in goods; and the price.

The SGA neither defines a contract nor sets out the requirements of a contract. These matters are dealt with by the common law. (See *Nutshell* on *Contract*.)

Goods are defined by s.61(1) as all personal chattels other than things in action and money. A **personal chattel** is a physical thing which can be touched and moved, such as a boat, a pen or a radio. Houses and land are not regarded as personal chattels. They are real property, not goods. However, crops and things attached to the land can be goods, as long as they are to be detached from the land either before the contract of sale or under its performance. A **thing in action** is an intangible right which can be enforced only by taking legal action. Examples would include patents, shares in a company or cheques.

As yet, the courts have not given a definite answer to the question whether or not **computer software** can be classified as goods. It seems reasonably clear that a personal chattel, such as a car, which has built in software will be regarded as goods. In the same way, a computer sold with software already installed on it will also be goods. When software is supplied on its own, it may be the case that this is a sale of goods if it is supplied on a floppy disk, as a floppy disk is a personal chattel, but not if it was downloaded from the Internet. The main reason for wanting to know whether or not software is goods is to establish the appropriate type of liability if it should turn out to be defective.

If software is goods, then when it is sold the SGA will govern the contract and s.14(2) will impose strict liability on the seller if the goods are defective. If software is not goods, then the sale of it will not be governed by the SGA and the common law liability of the seller is likely to be fault based. It seems somewhat strange to have different liability regimes, depending upon the way in which the software was supplied. It has therefore been suggested that the supply of software is a contract *sui generis* (in a class of its own). It remains to be seen whether or not the courts adopt this analysis. If they do, they could impose a liability regime which is specifically designed to be appropriate to the sale of software.

The **transfer of property in goods** means the transfer of ownership of goods. So a contract will not be within the Act unless it provides that ownership of the goods should pass to the buyer. This means that contracts of hire and of hire-purchase are not within the Act. (However, terms are implied into these types of contracts by two other statutes, as we shall see in the following chapter where contracts of hire and hire-purchase are defined.) A contract to provide a service, such as a contract to clean windows, will not be a contract of sale of goods because no ownership of goods is transferred. However, some contracts provide both goods and services. The fact that some goods are transferred does not automatically make the contract a sale of goods. The contract can still be a contract of service. The test which the courts use, to decide whether a contract is a sale of goods or a contract of service, is to decide what the essence of the contract was. Take, for example, a contract to service a car under which new engine oil is also supplied. The essence of this contract is that it is a contract to provide services. The supplying of the goods, the engine oil, is not the essence of the contract and so the SGA would not apply to the contract. Now consider a contract to buy four new tyres for a car, the tyres to be fitted by the seller. Here the essence of the contract is that it is a sale of goods, with the service element of the contract being relatively incidental. Therefore this contract would be a contract of sale of goods and the SGA would govern it. Case law on whether a contract is essentially one of sale of goods, or essentially one to provide a service, is not particularly helpful. Each case is decided on its own facts.

In order for a contract to be one of sale of goods, the buyer must pay a **money consideration called the price**. So if the goods are bartered for other goods, with no money changing hands, then the contract cannot be a sale of goods. Difficulties can arise where the two parties both transfer ownership of goods to each other, with a monetary adjustment to take account of one party's goods being worth more that the other's. In *Aldridge v Johnson* [1857] 32 bullocks, which the parties valued at £192, were exchanged along with £23 for 100 quarters of barley, which the parties valued at £215. This was regarded as two contracts of sale because the parties had given a definite price to both lots of goods. If the parties had merely exchanged the goods, and subsequently made a price adjustment, then neither contract would have been a sale of goods. *Esso Petroleum Ltd v Commisioners of Customs and Excise* [1976] considered the position where a "free gift" was supplied to motorists who bought four gallons of petrol. The House of Lords held that a motorist who received the "gift" had given some consideration for it, but this consideration had not been the payment of money. Rather, it was entering into the separate contract to buy four gallons of petrol. Consequently there was no sale of goods.

Finally, it should be noticed that there is no requirement that the seller should sell in the course of a business. However, if the seller does not sell in this way then two important statutory terms will not be implied into the contract. (See satisfactory quality and fitness for purpose in Ch.2.)

As we have already seen, if a contract cannot be classified as a contract of sale of goods then the SGA will not apply to that contract. One of the most important parts of the SGA, Part II, implies certain terms into contracts of sale of goods. In Chapter 2 we shall examine these terms in detail. We shall also see that identical terms are implied into contracts which cannot be classified as contracts of sale of goods, but under which goods pass. These identical terms are implied by other statutes. So if a contract cannot be classified as a contract of sale of goods two consequences will flow from this. First, the statutory implied terms will be implied by statutes other than the SGA. Second, the SGA will not govern the contract and, apart from the statutory implied terms, no other statute will make rules equivalent to those set out in the SGA.

Sale and agreement to sell

Where the property (ownership) in the goods is transferred to the buyer as soon as the contract is made, the contract is a sale of goods. (Section 2(4).) Where the property in the goods is to

take place at a future time, or subject to some condition, the
contract is an agreement to sell. (Section 2(5).) Both sales and
agreements to sell are regarded as contracts of sale of goods and
are therefore governed by the SGA.

Example

Alice buys a painting at an auction. The contract is made as
soon as Alice's bid is accepted by the auctioneer, and at this
moment ownership of the painting passes to Alice. This is
therefore a contract of sale. If the auction particulars had stated
that ownership of the goods would not pass until the goods had
been paid for, then this would have been an agreement to sell.
The contract would have been made as soon as the bid was
accepted, but ownership would not have passed until the
condition was fulfilled.

Specific, and unascertained goods

At the time of the contract the goods will be either specific or
unascertained. As we shall see in Ch.3, this distinction usually
determines the time at which ownership of the goods is transferred to the buyer. In the context of the passing of property in
the goods, it is therefore a very significant distinction. Section
61(1) defines **specific goods** as goods which are identified and
agreed upon at the time a contract of sale is made. This means
that both the buyer and the seller have identified and agreed
upon exactly which goods are being sold, so that no other goods
could be used to perform the contract. **Unascertained goods** are
not defined by the SGA but would include all goods which were
not specific. So, in effect, the definition of specific goods defines
unascertained goods by default.

Existing and future goods

Existing goods are goods which are either owned or possessed
by the seller. Future goods are goods which the seller has yet to
acquire or yet to manufacture. (Section 5(1).) Sales of both
existing and future goods are regarded as contracts of sale of
goods. It should be noticed that goods which do in fact exist are
not regarded as existing goods if the seller neither owns nor
possesses them. For example, Billy having agreed to buy a
painting from Charles, might then agree to sell this painting to

David. The painting does exist at the time of the contract between Billy and David but it is regarded by the SGA as future goods, rather than existing goods, because at the time of the contract Billy does not possess or own the painting. Where a seller contracts to sell future goods this must operate as an agreement to sell the goods. (Section 5(3).)

AN OVERVIEW OF THE SGA 1979

The original Sale of Goods Act was passed in 1893, codifying existing common law rules. The SGA 1979 consolidated the 1893 Act, making only minor changes. Since 1893 a large body of case law has clarified the meanings of the words used in the SGA.

Although the SGA 1893 codified the common law in so far as it relates to contracts of the sale of goods, the codification was not complete. For example, the Act applies only to contracts for the sale of goods but it does not deal with the way in which a contract is formed. Section 62(2) tells us that the rules of common law and equity apply to contracts for the sale of goods, unless these rules are inconsistent with a section of the Act. So if there is any conflict between a case and the Act, the Act will always prevail. But at the same time the Act leaves unchanged the general common law principles of the law of contract.

2. STATUTORY IMPLIED TERMS

OVERVIEW

Sections 12–15 of the Sale of Goods Act 1979 imply certain terms into **contracts of sale of goods**. These terms are as to:

the seller's right to sell;
correspondence with description;
satisfactory quality;
fitness for purpose; and
correspondence with sample.

Identical terms are implied into other types of contracts under which goods are transferred. However, these terms are not implied by the SGA but by two other statutes, depending upon how the contract is classified. It is therefore important to classify the contract so that we know which sections of which statutes imply the terms.

Three quite different terms are implied into **contracts to provide a service**. These terms are as to:

the use of reasonable care and skill;
that the service should be provided within a reasonable time (if no time was fixed); and
that the customer should pay a reasonable price (if no price was fixed).

These terms are implied into the relevant contract by ss.13–15 of the Supply of Goods and Services Act 1982. (The SGSA 1982.) If a contract is to supply both goods and services then both sets of terms, that is to say those relating to the supply of the services and those relating to the supply of the goods, will be implied.

The Unfair Contract Terms Act 1977 (UCTA 1977) restricts, or sometimes prevents, exclusion of the statutory implied terms. In addition, if the customer is a consumer, the Unfair Terms in Consumer Contracts Regulations 1999 might invalidate an unfair term.

CLASSIFICATION OF TRANSACTIONS

Contracts of sale of goods

In Ch.1 we examined the definition of a contract of sale of goods in some detail. If you have forgotten this definition you should go back and read it again. If a contract is a sale of goods then it is the SGA 1979 which will imply the statutory terms. Because the Sale of Goods Act was first passed before the other two statutes, in 1893, almost all of the case law relating to the meaning of the statutory implied terms was decided when considering contracts of sale of goods. (The other statutes which imply terms were first passed in the twentieth century.) These cases which consider the meaning of the SGA implied terms can be used to discover the meaning of the identical terms contained in the other two statutes.

Contracts of hire purchase

The statutory implied terms are implied into contracts of hire-purchase by ss.8–11 of the Supply of Goods (Implied Terms) Act 1973 (SGITA 1973). Under a hire-purchase contract goods are hired to a person who agrees to make periodical payments for the goods. In addition, the hirer is given **the option** to buy the goods at the end of the hire period in return for a nominal payment. The amount of this payment is usually included in the final instalment. A person taking goods under a hire-purchase agreement does not buy or agree to buy the goods. Rather, such a person has an option to buy the goods. For this reason the contract is not a sale of goods. (*Helby v Mathews* [1895].) A **conditional sale agreement** can be very similar. However, the difference is that under such an agreement there is no hire of goods. Rather there is a definite agreement to buy and sell the goods. The buyer makes a definite commitment to buy the goods but the contract provides that, although the buyer will get possession of the goods from the outset, ownership will not pass to the buyer until the final instalment is paid. As there is a definite agreement to buy, it is the SGA which implies the statutory terms into conditional sales. A **credit sale** is a sale of goods under which the buyer gets immediate ownership and possession of the goods but is given a period of credit by the seller. Such a sale is governed by the SGA.

Example

Tom, Dick and Harry all want to get motorbikes which they cannot afford. Tom enters into a contract of hire-purchase which is to run for a three year period. He gets immediate possession of the motorbike, but does not agree to pay all of the instalments for the full three years. If he does pay all of the instalments he will buy the motorbike for a nominal sum when he pays the final instalment. Dick makes a definite agreement to buy a motorbike, paying the price by instalments over three years. The contract provides that ownership of the motorbike will not pass until Dick has paid all of the instalments. Nevertheless, Dick takes possession as soon as the contract is made. This is a conditional sale agreement. Harry takes immediate possession, and gets immediate ownership, of his motorbike but the seller agrees that the price can be paid by instalments. This is a credit sale. The SGITA 1973 implies the statutory terms into Tom's contract. The SGA 1979 implies the terms into the contracts of Dick and Harry.

Contracts for the transfer of property (ownership) in goods

The statutory terms are implied into contracts for the transfer of property in goods by ss.2–5 SGSA 1982. Such contracts include all contracts under which ownership of goods is, or is to be, transferred, except contracts of sale of goods or hire-purchase.

Contracts of hire

The statutory terms are implied into contracts of hire by ss.7–10 of the SGSA 1982. A contract of hire is one under which a person is given possession of goods in return for payment. Under such a contract ownership is neither transferred nor agreed to be transferred. A contract of hire-purchase is not governed by the SGSA 1982 because, as we have seen, such a contract is governed by the SGITA 1973.

The terms implied by the various statutes are identical no matter how the transaction is classified. There is an argument that one statute should cater for all the different types of transactions. However, as yet, this has not happened and so the correct part of the correct statute must be used.

Example

Jill buys, or agrees to buy, a car from a garage. The SGA ss.12–15 imply the terms. If Jill had taken the car on hire-purchase, ss.8–11 SGITA 1973 would have implied the terms. If the contract had been some other type under which ownership in goods was transferred then ss.2–5 SGSA 1982 would have implied the terms. If the car had been hired to Jill then ss.7–10 SGSA 1982 would have done so. If the contract had been to have her car serviced, then a different set of terms would have been implied by ss.13–15 SGSA 1982.

The following figure gives an overview of the appropriate statutory sections.

FIGURE 2.1

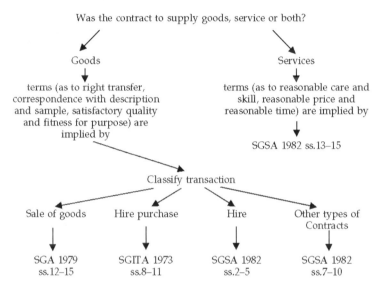

It is important to remember that if the contract is one under which goods are transferred, (whether under a sale of goods, hire, hire-purchase or otherwise), it might also be one under which services are supplied. If so then, in addition to the implied terms relating to the goods, terms will be implied in relation to the service element of the contract. These terms will be implied by ss.13–15 SGSA 1982, which is considered at the end of this chapter.

We now consider the terms implied by the SGA 1979 and indicate which sections of the SGITA 1973 and the SGSA 1982 imply the identical terms.

IMPLIED TERMS ABOUT TITLE

Section 12 SGA sets out three terms about title. These terms are implied whether or not the seller sells the goods in the course of a business. The first of these, a condition that the seller has the right to sell the goods, is much more important than the other two terms, which are warranties (as to quiet possession and freedom from encumbrances).

THE RIGHT TO SELL (SGA s.12(1))

Section 12(1) SGA provides that there is an implied condition on the part of the seller that in the case of a sale he has the right to sell the goods. If the contract is an agreement to sell it is implied that the seller will have the right to sell at the time when the property is to pass. So a seller of future goods will not breach s.12(1) merely because he does not yet own the goods. A sale of future goods operates as an agreement to sell, as we saw in Ch.1, and so s.12(1) requires only that the seller will have the right to sell at the time when the property is to pass.

Example

On January 5 a dealer agrees to sell a painting which he has himself agreed to buy from a museum. The contract states that the property is to pass from the dealer to the buyer on March 1. The dealer will not breach s.12(1) merely because he cannot pass ownership to the buyer at the time of the contract. The dealer will breach s.12(1) if he cannot pass ownership on March 1.

Section 12(3) provides that the seller can protect himself by making it plain that he is selling only whatever title he or a third party might have. For example, a seller who did not know if he owned certain goods could sell such ownership as he might have. If it turned out that he had no ownership s.12(1) would not have been breached.

Generally, a breach of s.12(1) will occur because the seller does not own the goods which he has sold or agreed to sell. Notice, however, that there is no requirement that the seller should know that he does not own the goods. In the leading case, *Rowland v Divall* [1923] a dealer breached s.12(1) because he sold a car which had been stolen before he got it. The dealer did not know this, and could not reasonably have been expected to know it, but he nevertheless breached s.12(1).

It is possible for s.12(1) to be breached even where the seller does own the goods. For example, in *Niblett v Confectioners Materials* [1921] a manufacturer of condensed milk sold 1000 tins of such milk which were labelled "Nissly Brand". Nestle, the milk and chocolate manufacturer, could have prevented the resale of these tins because the word "Nissly" was too similar to the Nestle trademark. Even though the sellers owned the milk when they sold it, they were in breach of s.12(1). This was because they had no right to sell the milk in the tins bearing the offending label

Consequences of breach of s.12(1)

Section 12(1) is a condition. (Section 12(5A).) If a condition of a contract is breached then the injured party has the right to treat the contract as terminated. However, when the contract is a contract of sale of goods, a buyer who has 'accepted' the goods can no longer terminate for breach of a condition but can only claim damages for breach of warranty. (Section 11(4).) The ways in which a contract can be accepted are examined in detail in Ch.6. In *Rowland v Divall* it was held that the right to terminate for breach of s.12(1) cannot be lost on account of the buyer having accepted the goods. If this view is correct, it makes the remedy for a breach of s.12(1) different from the remedies available for breach of the other statutory implied terms which are classed as conditions.

When a buyer terminates a contract of sale of goods, on account of the seller having breached a condition, then owner-ship of the goods reverts to the seller and the buyer must make the goods available to the seller. The buyer can then claim the price back on account of a there having been a total failure of consideration. If a buyer had had extensive use of the goods then this would be unfair as the buyer would still get the whole of the purchase price back. Section 11(4) caters for this by stating that a buyer who has "accepted" the goods cannot reject for breach of condition but must treat the breach of condition as a breach of warranty. As we shall see in Ch.6, a buyer who has had extensive use of the goods will be deemed to have accepted the goods and will therefore no longer be able to reject them and reclaim the price. In *Rowland v Divall* the dealer who sold the car which he did not own had had the use of the car for some months. Nevertheless it was held that the car could not have been accepted because when s.12(1) is breached, and no title is passed to the seller, this always amounts to a total failure of consideration. This view has been criticised but still repres-ents the law. It is based on the idea that a buyer of goods buys the goods to own them, not just to use them. So if ownership never passed to the buyer then he did not get anything for which he paid the price. When goods bought for consumption have been totally consumed, it must be queried whether the buyer who has consumed them has indeed suffered a total failure of consideration. For example, if a buyer of a sack of potatoes eats all of them and them discovers that the seller of the potatoes did not own them, has the buyer really suffered a total failure of consideration? *Rowland v Divall* would hold that he had and that he would be entitled to a refund of all of the purchase price. The true owner of the potatoes could sue either the buyer or the seller (or the thief) for damages in the tort of conversion. If the true owner sued the seller then the seller would lose twice, whereas the buyer would have got the potatoes for nothing. The seller would have paid the thief for the potatoes, got nothing from the buyer, and have to pay damages to the true owner. The buyer would have eaten the potatoes and recovered the full price from the seller. But, on the other hand, if the true owner sued the buyer then the position would seem to be much fairer. The difficulty is that the true owner is more likely to sue the seller, as an earlier person in the chain, than to sue the buyer. An answer might be provided by the Civil Liability (Contribution) Act 1978. As both buyer and seller are potentially liable to the owner in conversion, whichever of them was sued by the owner could use the Act to claim an indemnity or contribution from the one who was not sued.

Warranties as to quiet possession and freedom from encumbrances (SGA s.12(2))

Section 12(2) implies warranties as to quiet possession and as to freedom from encumbrances. As these terms are classified only as warranties, breach of them will not entitle the buyer to treat the contract as terminated but only to claim damages.

The term as to freedom from encumbrances will be breached if the goods sold are subject to an encumbrance such as a charge, a mortgage or a lien.

The term as to quiet possession is to the effect that the buyer will not be prevented from enjoying his use of the goods by anybody else. This warranty continues after the property has passed to the buyer. (*Microbeads SA v Vinhurst Road Markings Ltd* [1975].)

Which statutory sections imply the terms?

Sale of goods	Right to sell	SGA 1979 s.12(1)
	The warranties	SGA 1979 s.12(2)

Hire-purchase	Right to sell	SGITA 1973 s.8(1)(a)
	The warranties	SGITA 1973 s.8(1)(b)
Transfer of property	Right to sell	SGSA 1982 s.2(1)
	The warranties	SGSA 1982 s.2(2)
Hire	Right to sell	SGSA 1982 s.7(1)
	The warranties	SGSA 1982 s.7(2)

CORRESPONDENCE WITH DESCRIPTION (SGA s.13(1))

Section 13(1) SGA states that where there is a contract for the sale of goods by description, there is an implied condition that the goods correspond with the description. This is the case whether or not the seller sells the goods in the course of a business. Originally, it was only unascertained or future goods which could be sold by description but for many years it has been the case that specific goods can also be sold by description.

The descriptive words must be terms

Section 13(1) will apply only if the description is intended to be a term of the contract. If the description is intended to have no legal effect, or is merely a representation, then s.13 will not apply. Descriptions made before the formation of a contract will be terms if the parties intended them to be a part of the contract. They will be representations if the parties did not intend them to be part of the contract. If a representation is untrue there might be a remedy for misrepresentation (see *Nutshell on Contract*) but there will be no breach of s.13 SGA.

The goods must be sold by reference to the description

The goods must be sold by reference to the description. So the description must be relied upon by the buyer. If it was not reasonably intended that the buyer would rely on the description then the description will not be within s.13. (*Harlingdon & Leinster Ltd v Christopher Hull Fine Art Ltd* [1991].) When unascertained goods are sold in a commercial context it is presumed that the buyer does rely on any description of them.

The description must identify the kind of goods being sold

A description will be within s.13 only if it identifies the kind of goods which are being bought. (*Reardon Smith Lines v Hansen*

Tangen [1976] and *Ashington Piggeries v Christopher Hill Ltd* [1972].) Words which merely identify which particular goods are being bought will not do. To be within s.13 the words must be a substantial ingredient in the identity of the thing being sold. (*Reardon Smith.*) However, when unascertained goods are sold in bulk it is more likely that s.13 will require exact correspondence with all aspects of the description. This was certainly the old approach in cases such as *Re Moore and Landeur & Co* [1921]. In that case a purchase of 3,100 cans of peaches could be rejected under s.13 because some of the cans were packed in cases of 24, whereas the contract description said that they would all be packed in cases of 30. In *Reardon Smith* Lord Wilberforce said that some of the old cases were excessively technical and due for a fresh examination. However, since the introduction of s.15A, considered below in relation to remedies for breach of s.13, the injustice in cases such as *Re Moore* could be removed whilst still holding that s.13 had been breached.

True significance of s.13 is that it is a condition

Terms can be classified as either conditions, warranties or innominate terms. A condition is a very important term, which goes to the root of the contract. A warranty is a less important term which does not go to the root of the contract. If a warranty is breached the injured party can claim damages but cannot terminate the contract. If a condition is breached the injured party can both claim damages and terminate the contract. When deciding whether or not a term is a condition or a warranty the court considers whether the parties thought that the term went to the root of the contract **at the time when they made the contract**. Innominate terms adopt a different approach. The test to decide whether breach of an innominate terms allows termination of the contract is to ask whether the breach which actually occurred **deprived the injured party of substantially the whole intended benefit of the contract**. If the breach did not do this, the only remedy is damages. If the breach did do this, then both damages and termination of the contract are available. (These matters are considered in more detail in *Nutshell on Contract.*)

We have seen that a description must be a term of the contract in order to be within s.13. But not all terms of the contract are within s.13. To be within s.13, the goods must also be sold by reference to the descriptive term and the term must identify the kind of thing being sold. An express term which is not within s.13 might be a warranty or an innominate term. But a term which is within s.13 is a condition because s.13 is stated by the s.13(1A) to be a condition. So the true significance of s.13 is that any term within s.13 **is** a condition, whereas a descriptive term which is not within s.13 **might** be a condition, but equally might be a warranty or an innominate term.

Section 13(3) provides that goods can be sold by description if they are exposed for sale and selected by a buyer, as happens in self-service shops.

The modern approach to s.13 is that it is not concerned with the quality of the goods or with their fitness for purpose. Both of these matters are dealt with by s.14. However, when goods sold by description are contaminated it can be difficult to decide when this moves from being a quality issue to being a failure to match the contract description. For example, in *Pinnock Bros v Lewis and Peat Ltd* [1923] copra cake was so adulterated with castor beans that it could no longer be said to correspond with its description as copra cake. Whereas in *Ashington Piggeries* herring meal which was only slightly contaminated still corresponded with its description as herring meal.

Remedies for breach of s.13(1) (and ss.14(2), 14(3) and 15)

As s.13(1) is a condition, the buyer can (subject to s.15A below) treat the contract as repudiated if it is breached. If the buyer does elect to treat the contract as repudiated the goods must be made available for collection by the seller and the buyer can bring an action for damages for non-delivery under s.51, as well as reclaiming the price. The action for non-delivery is available because, although the goods might have been delivered, delivery was undone when the buyer exercised his right to treat the contract as repudiated. The buyer does not need to treat the contract as repudiated and can instead elect to treat the breach of condition as a breach of warranty. (Section 11(2).) A buyer who elects to do this will not be able to reclaim the price, nor be able to claim damages for non-delivery. Instead the buyer will be able to claim damages for breach of warranty under s.53.

Section 15A provides that where there is a breach of ss.13 a buyer who does not deal as a consumer will have to treat the breach as a breach of warranty **if the breach is so slight that it would be unreasonable for the buyer to reject the goods.** This section does not state that a buyer who does deal as a consumer will be able to reject the goods for any breach of ss.13–15, even if the breach is so slight that rejection would be unreasonable. However, it does imply this. (The SGA definition of "dealing as a consumer" is considered later in this chapter in relation to the Unfair Contract Terms Act 1977.)

Example

Sid, a shopkeeper, buys a torch from a wholesaler. The contract is breached because the goods do not match the contract description but the breach is so slight that it would be unreasonable for Sid to reject the goods. Sid sells the torch to Charles, a consumer, repeating the description which was made to him. Section 13 has been breached as regards both contracts. Charles could treat the contract as repudiated because he dealt as a consumer. Sid could not treat the contract with the wholesaler as repudiated but could claim damages for breach of warranty.

Section 15A applies not only to s.13, but to ss.14 and 15 as well. It does not apply to s.12(1). Whenever s.12(1) is breached any buyer, whether dealing as a consumer or not, will have the right to treat the contract as terminated. Section 15A does not apply to s.12(2) because the terms implied by s.12(2) are warranties, rather than conditions.

When we considered s.12(1) we saw that the right to reject for its breach cannot be lost on account of the buyer having accepted the goods. Section 13, like ss.14 and 15, is different. Section 11(4) provides that a buyer who has "accepted" goods will no longer be able to reject them for breach of condition, but will have to treat the breach of condition as a breach of warranty. This is an important rule. The ways in which a buyer can be deemed to have accepted the goods are considered in detail in Ch.6.

Which statutory sections imply the term?

Sale of goods	SGA s.13(1)
Hire-purchase	SGITA 1973 s.9(1)
Transfer of property	SGSA 1982 s.3(2)
Hire	SGSA 1982 s.8(2)

TERMS IMPLIED ONLY INTO SALES MADE IN THE COURSE OF A BUSINESS

Section 14 implies two terms into contracts where the seller sells goods in the course of a business. The terms implied by ss.12 and 13 are not limited in this way. The terms implied by s.14 are that the goods should be of satisfactory quality (s.14(2)) and that they should be fit for the buyer's purpose (s.14(3)).

Meaning of selling goods in the course of a business

In *Stevenson v Rogers* [1999] the Court of Appeal held that whenever a business sells anything then, **for the purposes of s.14**, it does so in the course of a business. This landmark decision changed the previous law. In the case a commercial fisherman sold a fishing boat. It was held that the sale was made in the course of the fisherman's business even though the sale was only incidental to the fisherman's business. There was no need to show that the selling of boats was an integral part of the business or that the business had sold boats before.

Stevenson v Rogers is generally the starting point for any question relating to either of the two terms implied by s.14. If the goods were not sold in the course of a business then s.14 will not imply terms into the contract. Furthermore, apart from the two terms implied by ss.14(2) and (3), terms as to quality or fitness for purpose are not implied into contracts of sale. (Section 14(1).) Such terms may, of course, be expressly agreed by the parties.

SATISFACTORY QUALITY (SGA s.14(2))

Section 14(2) implies a condition that where the seller sells goods in the course of a business the goods are of satisfactory quality. Before we examine the meaning of satisfactory quality we should notice two specific circumstances in which the term will not be implied.

Circumstances in which the term as to satisfactory quality will not be implied

Section 14(2C) sets out two circumstances in which the term as to satisfactory quality will not be implied, even if the seller does sell the goods in the course of a business.

Section 14(2C)(a) provides that the term implied by s.14(2) does not extend to any matter making the quality of goods unsatisfactory which is specifically drawn to the buyer's attention before the contract is made. The use of the word "specifically" shows that sellers will not be protected by generalised statements, such as that there might be something wrong with the goods. In order to be protected the particular defect which renders the goods unsatisfactory must be specifically drawn to the buyer's attention.

Section 14(2C)(b) provides that the term implied by s.14(2) does not extend to any matter making the quality of goods unsatisfactory where the buyer examines the goods before the contract is made, and that examination ought to have revealed the defect. So if the buyer examines the goods and the examination ought to have revealed a particular defect in the goods then the buyer cannot later claim that that particular defect rendered the goods unsatisfactory. However, it should be noticed that the buyer has no obligation to examine the goods. So, as far as s.14(2) is concerned, a buyer who does not examine the goods at all might well find himself in a better position than a buyer who does. It should also be noticed that the type of defects which a buyer who examines the goods might be expected to discover will depend upon the thoroughness of the examination. If a buyer of a second-hand car gave it a cursory look over before buying it from a garage the examination might be expected to reveal very obvious defects, such as extensive corrosion of the bodywork. If the buyer got underneath the car and gave the chassis a thorough examination this might be expected to reveal even small patches of corrosion, as long as they could be seen by the naked eye. However, see *Bramhill v Edwards* [2004], considered below in relation to the meaning of satisfactory quality.

The definition of satisfactory quality

Section 14(2A) states that goods are of satisfactory quality if they meet the standard that a reasonable person would regard as satisfactory, taking account of any description of the goods, the price (if relevant) and all the other relevant circumstances.

It is perhaps best to take this definition in two stages. First, a straightforward objective test is set out. Goods are of satisfactory quality if a reasonable person would think so. Not the particular buyer or the particular seller, or a reasonable buyer or a reasonable seller, just a reasonable person. However, this reasonable person will be credited with the background knowledge which the parties to the contract might be expected to have.

The second part of the definition lists three matters which should be taken into account: any description of the goods; the price; and all the other relevant circumstances. We should notice that here it is **any** description of the goods. There is no need that the description should have been one by which the goods were sold, as there was in relation to s.13. The price is often likely to be a highly relevant circumstance. If I bought a second-hand car from a garage for £5,000 the reasonable person would expect its quality to be far higher than a similar make and model of car sold for £1,000. Finally, any other circumstance, such as that a car was sold for scrap rather than to be driven, will be taken into account.

Aspects of quality in appropriate cases

It should not be forgotten that it is s.14(2A) which sets out the definition of satisfactory quality. Section 14(2B) sets out five **aspects of quality in appropriate cases**. Very commonly these aspects of quality are given far more importance than they merit. It should be noticed that they are not absolute requirements and in some cases none of the five matters listed will be appropriate. This can be seen if we again consider a car sold for scrap. If the car had been badly damaged it might well be lacking in all of the five matters listed. However, the reasonable person could still conclude that it was of satisfactory quality. By contrast, in *Clegg v Olle Andersson* [2003] Lady Justice Hale said that new, high-priced, quality products should be free from even minor defects. They should be perfect or nearly so.

Bearing in mind that they are **only aspects of quality in appropriate cases**, the matters listed in s.14(2B) are as follows.

(a) **Fitness for all the purposes for which goods of the kind in question are commonly supplied.** Previously, goods were of merchantable quality as long as they were fit for at least one of their common purposes.

(b) **Appearance and finish.** In *Rogers v Parish Ltd* [1987] a new Range Rover with several teething troubles, (such as scratches on the paint work, leaking oil seals and excessive engine noise,) was held not to be of merchantable quality. If such a case were to arise today it seems likely that it would hardly be worth arguing that the car was of satisfactory quality.

(c) **Freedom from minor defects.** This aspect of quality would change *Millars of Falkirk v Turpie* [1976], where a new car with a defective steering system was held to be merchantable because the fault could easily be fixed.

(d) **Safety.** It is important to remember here that safety is only an aspect of quality in appropriate cases. If a car was sold very cheaply for spare parts it might well be unsafe to drive but this would not mean that the car was not of satisfactory quality.

(e) **Durability.** The goods must be reasonably durable when supplied. If the goods deteriorate after they have been bought the buyer must prove that they were not durable when supplied. The following, Scottish, case shows the difficulties which a buyer might face. In *Thain v Anniesland Trade Centre* [1997] a six year old Renault 19 was bought for £2,995. The car had done 80,000 miles and a new version would have cost about £11,000. The claimant did not buy a three month warranty which she was offered. Soon after the car was bought it's gearbox began to make a noise. It soon became apparent that the gearbox would need to be replaced and this was uneconomic in a car of this age. The car was held to be of satisfactory quality. The sheriff principal held that the problem was not present at the time when the car was sold, (it had been examined by several knowledgeable drivers,) and that the reasonable person would not have expected this particular car to be durable. As the case is Scottish, it is of persuasive authority only. Most commentators think that the same decision would have been reached by an English court.

Public statements about the characteristics of the goods

If the buyer deals as a consumer the relevant circumstances referred to in the s.14(2A) definition of satisfactory quality include any public statements about the characteristics of the goods made by the seller, the producer or his representative, particularly in advertising or labelling. (Section14(2E).) However, this is not the case if the seller can prove:

(a) that he could not have been aware of the statement at the time the contract was made; or

(b) that the statement had been publicly withdrawn or corrected before the contract was made; or

(c) that the consumer's decision to buy the goods could not have been influenced by the public statement.

It should be noticed that s.14(2E) makes a public statement a relevant circumstance only where the buyer deals as a consumer. The definition of dealing as a consumer is complex and is considered later in this chapter when we consider possible exclusion of the statutory implied terms.

Strict liability

Liability under s.14(2) SGA is strict. That is to say it arises merely because goods which are not of satisfactory quality have been sold in the course of a business. There is no requirement that the seller is at fault in any way. For example, if a shop sells a pre-packaged television set which is faulty then the shop will be liable even if it could not have known of this fault.

Cases on the requirement of satisfactory quality

There have been very few cases which expand upon the meaning of the requirement of satisfactory quality. In *Jewson Ltd v Kelly* [2003] Sedley L.J. said that, "Section 14(2) is directed principally to the sale of substandard goods. This means that the court's principal concern is to look at their intrinsic quality, using the tests indicated in subsection (2A) (2B) and (2C)." He went on to say that if the buyer wanted to use the goods for a purpose which was not predictable this would be relevant to s.14(3) rather than to s.14(2). He gave an example of a soft toy. If the toy was given to a toddler and injured the toddler's mouth then s.14(2) would be likely to have been breached, safety and durability being appropriate aspects of quality. But if the toy was given to a dog and injured the dog's mouth then s.14(2) would be unlikely to have been breached, unless the toy was bought in a pet shop.

Case example. *Bramhill v Edwards* [2004]. The claimant bought an American motor home from a UK dealer for £61,000. Six months later he discovered that the motor home was illegal for use on UK roads because it was 102 inches wide, the legal limit being 100 inches. The claimant informed the dealer of this but continued to use the motor home for the next four months. Then he took legal proceedings. The Court of Appeal overturned the trial judge in holding that the motor home was of satisfactory quality. The reasonable person referred to in s.14(2A) was a reasonable person in the position of the buyer and attributed with knowledge of all relevant background facts. The claimant in this case was knowledgeable about motor homes and knew that the authorities turned a blind eye to the illegality and that the illegality did not prevent the motor home from being used or insured. Nor did it reduce the value of the motor home. The court put considerable emphasis on the burden of proof being on the claimant. It also said that what had to be proved was that "a reasonable person in the position of the buyer and with his knowledge of the background facts 'would' not regard the goods as unsatisfactory." The Court of Appeal also considered, obiter, whether s.14(2C)(b), considered above, would have applied as a defence to the requirement of satisfactory quality. The motor home had been sold "as seen". Furthermore, the claimant had thoroughly inspected the interior of the motor home and had lived in it for a few days before buying it. The trial judge thought that this examination ought to have revealed the width and the width was not revealed only because the claimant did not measure the motor home. He also said that the claimant should have appreciated, without measuring it, that the width was over the legal limit. The Court of Appeal upheld these views. It also seemed to think that there would have been a defence under s.14(2C)(a), which was not pleaded. This defence arose because the defendant had represented that the interior width was 100 inches and so the claimant should have realised that the exterior was at least 102 inches wide.

FITNESS FOR PURPOSE (SGA s.14(3))

As we have already seen, s.14(3) implies a term only where the seller sells goods in the course of a business. *Stevenson v Rogers* [1999], considered above in relation to s.14(2), applies equally to s.14(3). So whenever a business sells any goods the sale will, for the purposes of s.14(3), have been made in the course of the seller's business.

The term implied by s.14(3) is a condition that the goods supplied under the contract are reasonably fit for any purpose which the buyer expressly or impliedly made known to the seller. This is the case even if the purpose made known is not a purpose for which such goods are commonly supplied.

Example

Parvinder buys a printer from a shop and tells the shopkeeper that she wants to connect the printer to her Apple computer. The shopkeeper does not describe the goods or make any claims about its suitability. The printer will not work when connected to Parvinder's computer because it is compatible only with PCs. The condition contained in s.14(3) has been breached, even though there is nothing inherently wrong with the printer.

Circumstances in which s.14(3) will not apply

First, as we have seen, s.14(3) will not apply unless the seller makes the contract in the course of a business.

Second, the term will not apply unless the buyer actually makes known to the seller the particular purpose for which the goods are being bought. The buyer can do this expressly or impliedly. But the term will not be implied if the buyer does not make the particular purpose known. In the example above, if Parvinder had not indicated to the shopkeeper that the printer was to be used with an Apple computer then the term would not have been breached.

Third, the term does not apply if the circumstances show either that the buyer did not rely on the skill and judgment of the seller or that it was unreasonable for the buyer to do this. So if the seller, in the example above, had known that Parvinder was an expert dealer in computers, and if Parvinder had done no more than mention that the printer was to be used with an Apple computer, then the term might not have been implied. The term can apply if the buyer makes only a partial reliance on the seller's skill and judgment. (*Ashington Piggeries Ltd v Christopher Hill Ltd* [1971].)

A buyer who buys goods for their usual purpose will be taken to have made known the purpose for which the goods were bought, and also to have relied on the seller's skill and judgment to have selected his stock with care and skill. (*Grant v Australian Knitting Mills Ltd* [1936].) When a buyer buys goods the poor quality of which means that they cannot be used for their usual purpose then both ss.14(2) and 14(3) are likely to have been breached.

Liability under s.14(3), like liability under s.14(2) is **strict** rather than fault based.

Remedies for breach of s.14

Earlier in this chapter we considered the remedies for a breach
of s.13(1). The same rules apply to a breach of either s.14(2) or
s.14(3). So if you read the part of the text dealing with remedies
for breach of s.13(1) you will see that s.11(4) will compel a buyer
who has 'accepted' the goods to treat a breach of condition as a
breach of warranty. You will also see that s.15A will force a
buyer who does not deal as a consumer to treat a breach of
condition as a breach of warranty if the breach of the term is so
slight that it would be unreasonable to reject.

Which statutory sections imply the terms?

Sale of goods	satisfactory quality	SGA s.14(2)
	fitness for purpose	SGA s.14(3)
Hire-purchase	satisfactory quality	SGITA 1973 s.10(2)
	fitness for purpose	SGITA 1973 s.10(3)
Transfer of property	satisfactory quality	SGSA 1982 s.4(2)
	fitness for purpose	SGSA 1982 s.4(5)
Hire	satisfactory quality	SGSA 1982 s.9(2)
	fitness for purpose	SGSA 1982 s.9(5)

TERMS IMPLIED INTO SALES BY SAMPLE (SECTION 15(2))

Meaning of a sale by sample

Section 15(1) tells us that a contract of sale is a contract of sale
by sample if there is an express or implied term saying that it is.
In *Drummond v Van Ingen* (1887) Lord MacNaghton said that a
sample was meant to give a visual meaning to the true intentions of the parties. He recognised that a sample might show
that which would be very difficult to describe in words.

Terms implied into a sale by sample

Section 15(2)(a) implies a term that the bulk will correspond to
the sample in quality. This term is rather like s.13, with the

sample taking the place of the description by which the goods were sold. It should be noticed that a contract can be both a sale by description and a sale by sample. If this is the case, then both s.13(1) and s.15(2) will imply conditions into the contract. Like s.13(1), s.15(2)(a) applies even if the seller does not make the contract in the course of a business.

Section 15(2)(c) implies a condition that the goods will be free from any defect making their quality unsatisfactory if this defect would not be apparent on a reasonable examination of the sample. Section 14(2), as we have seen, requires goods sold in the course of a business to be of satisfactory quality. We have also seen that s.14(2) does not require the buyer to examine the goods, but that if the buyer does examine them then any defect which this examination ought to have revealed will not make the goods of unsatisfactory quality. The whole purpose of a sample is that a buyer examines it. So the effect of s.15(2)c) is that it regards the buyer as having examined the sample. If the bulk of the goods contain a defect making them of unsatisfactory quality the position will depend upon whether this defect would have been apparent on a reasonable examination of the sample. If it would have been apparent, then neither s.14(2) nor s.15(2)c) will have been breached, even if the buyer did not examine the sample or notice the defect. (Section 14(2C(c) makes it plain that s.14(2) will not have been breached.) If it would not have been apparent, then s.15(2)c) will have been breached.

Case example. *Godley v Perry* [1960]. A newsagent sold a catapult to a boy. When used by the boy the catapult snapped and knocked the boy's eye out. The shopkeeper was liable to the boy under s.14(2). The newsagent had bought the catapults by sample from a wholesaler, and his wife had tested a sample catapult by pulling the elastic back. This catapult did not snap. The wholesaler was liable for breach of s.15(2)c).

Remedies for breach of s.15(2)

The remedies are the same as for a breach of s.13(1) and you should read the heading in this chapter which dealt with those remedies.

Which statutory sections imply the terms?

Sale of goods	correspondence with sample	SGA s.14(2)
	freedom from apparent defects	SGA s.14(3)

Hire-purchase	correspondence with sample	SGITA 1973 s.11(1)(a)
	freedom from apparent defects	SGITA 1973 s.11(1)(c)
Transfer of property	correspondence with sample	SGSA 1982 s.5(2)(a)
	freedom from apparent defects	SGSA 1982 s.5(2)c)
Hire	correspondence with sample	SGSA 1982 s.10(2)(a)
	freedom from apparent defects	SGSA 1982 s.10(2)(c)

TERMS IMPLIED INTO CONTRACTS FOR THE SUPPLY OF A SERVICE. (SGSA 1982 SS.13–15.)

All of the implied terms considered so far in this chapter relate to goods. Part II of the SGSA 1982 implies three quite different terms into contracts for the supply of a service. These contracts are defined by SGSA s.12(1) as contracts under which a person agrees to carry out a service.

The most important of the terms is implied by s.13. This provides that in a contract for the supply of a service where the supplier is acting in the course of a business, **there is an implied term that the supplier will carry out the service with reasonable care and skill**. You should notice that this particular term applies only where the service is to be carried out in the course of a business. It will not apply otherwise. However, the term implied by s.13(1) was merely a codification of the common law and the common law can still require a lesser standard of care and skill from a person who supplied a service otherwise than in the course of a business. Earlier we saw that s.14 SGA 1979 imposes strict liability on a seller, who can be liable without being at fault in any way. The term implied by s.13 SGSA is quite different. The standard required is the **tort standard** of reasonable care and skill and a supplier who is not at fault will not breach the term.

The term as to reasonable care and skill does not necessarily mean that the supplier of the service guarantees that the service will achieve a desired result. In *Thake v Maurice* [1986] a doctor performed a vasectomy which naturally reversed itself. The doctor had not been negligent in carrying out the operation and so he was not liable. Of course, if the doctor had expressly guaranteed that the vasectomy would have worked then he would have been liable for breach of this express term.

Effect of breach of s.13 SGSA

The term implied by s.13 SGSA is not a condition or a warranty, but an **innominate term**. Any breach of the term will entitle the injured party to damages. However, termination of the contract will be allowed only if the breach deprived the injured party of substantially the whole benefit of the contract. (See *Nutshell on Contract*.)

Section 14(1) SGSA provides that where a service is to be supplied by a supplier who is acting in the course of a business there is an implied term that the service **should be supplied within a reasonable time**. What is a reasonable time is a question of fact. (Section 14(2).) Section 14(1) will not imply the term if the time for the performance of the service has been fixed by the contract or determined by a course of dealing between the parties.

Section 15(1) SGSA applies whether or not the service was supplied in the course of a business. It implies a term that **the supplier will be paid a reasonable charge** for the service. What is a reasonable charge is a question of fact. (Section 15(2).) Section 15(1) will not imply the term if the price has been fixed by the contract or determined by a course of dealing between the parties. It commonly happens that the price of a service is fixed by a course of dealings. If a business provides a service to a customer regularly, and always charges the same price, then this price will remain the price unless there is some agreement that it has changed.

Section 13 SGSA operating in conjunction with terms applying to goods

We have seen that the SGA implies terms into contracts of sale of goods and that SGITA 1973 and SGSA 1982 imply identical terms into other types of contracts under which goods pass. We have also seen that s.13 SGSA 1982 implies a completely different type of term into contracts to provide a service. Many contracts are to sell or supply goods, with a slight service element. Others are essentially contracts to supply services but goods are also incidentally sold or supplied. In such cases both s.13 SGSA and the relevant terms relating to goods will be implied.

Example

Alice goes to a garage and agrees to have four new tyres fitted to her car. The essence of this contract would be that it is a contract of sale of goods. If the tyres themselves were not of satisfactory quality then s.14(2) SGA would have been breached. If the tyres were fitted in a negligent way then s.13 SGSA would have been breached. If the tyres were not of satisfactory quality and were fitted negligently then both statutory implied terms would have been breached.

UCTA 1977 RULES ON EXCLUSION OF THE STATUTORY IMPLIED TERMS

In this chapter we have seen that three statutes imply terms into contracts. A seller or supplier might try to exclude these terms. In some cases this will be possible but in others it will not.

Terms which can never be excluded

The terms as to the right to sell, set out in s.12 SGA and the corresponding sections of SGITA 1973 and SGSA 1982, can never be excluded. (Sections 6 and 7 UCTA 1977.) However, as we saw when considering s.12(1) SGA, s.12(3) provides that a seller may contract to sell only such title as he or a third party might have.

Terms which can be excluded only in non-consumer contracts

In several sections of the SGA a distinction is made between a buyer who deals as a consumer and one who does not. This distinction is vitally important when considering exclusion of ss.13–15 SGA (and exclusion of the corresponding terms in SGITA 1973 and SGSA 1982). This is because when the customer does deal as a consumer these implied terms cannot be excluded by any contract term, whereas when a customer does not deal as a consumer it is possible that they can be. The circumstances in which the implied terms can be excluded is considered after consideration of the meaning of "deals as a consumer".

When does a buyer deal as a consumer?

Section 61(5A) SGA directs us to the Unfair Contract Terms Act 1977 to discover the meaning of "dealing as a consumer". It also tells us that it is up to the seller to prove that the buyer did not deal as a consumer.

Section 12(1) UCTA defines dealing as a consumer but in doing so makes a distinction between cases where the buyer is an individual and cases where the buyer is a company.

If the **buyer is an individual** then only two conditions need to be satisfied for the buyer to deal as a consumer. First, the buyer must neither make the contract in the course of a business nor hold himself out as doing so. Second, the seller must make the contract in the course of a business.

This definition seems straightforward enough. However, it is complicated by the fact that **in this context** "in the course of a business" does not have the straightforward meaning given to it by *Stevenson v Rogers* [1999]. When we considered s.14(2) SGA, earlier in this chapter, we saw that *Stevenson v Rogers* held that whenever a business sold anything it did so in the course of a business, **for the purposes of s.14 SGA**. Unfortunately, *Stevenson v Rogers* does not apply when considering the meaning of "in the course of a business" to determine whether or not a buyer deals as a consumer. Instead, the test set out in *R & B Customs Brokers Ltd v United Dominions Trust Ltd* [1988] is used. This test regards a buyer or seller as acting in the course of a business only if the contract is an integral part of the business. A contract will be made as an integral part of the business in only three circumstances. First, if the goods bought or sold are bought are the type of goods which the business is in business to buy or sell. (But not if the goods were merely necessary to allow the business to be carried on.) For example, if a taxi driver sold the first taxi he had used in the business this sale would not have been made in the course of the taxi driver's business. Second, if goods are bought or sold as a one-off adventure in the nature of trade. This is an expression used by the Inland Revenue and means that the goods were bought and sold with the intention of making a profit. Third, if the goods bought or sold are a type of goods which the business has bought or sold with some degree of regularity. In *R & B Customs Brokers* a business bought a car but was nevertheless dealing as a consumer. This was because the business was not in business to buy cars and it had not bought cars sufficiently regularly for the buying of cars to have become an integral part of its business. It must be said that it does seem unfortunate to have two different tests to determine the meaning of 'in the course of a business' depending upon where in a statute the expression is used.

Nevertheless, in *Feldarol Foundries plc v Hermes Leasing (London) Ltd* [2004] the Court of Appeal confirmed that this was the true position. It must also be pointed out that the effect of *Stevenson v Rogers* and *R & B Customs Brokers* is to increase consumer protection. Section 14 SGA protects consumers who buy goods from a business and a very wide test is used to determine whether the goods were sold in the course of business. Sections 6 and 7 UCTA 1977 protect consumers as long as they do not buy in the course of their business. A much narrower test is used here and so more (business) consumers are protected.

If the buyer is not an individual but is a company then a third requirement is added. This requirement is that the goods supplied under the contract are of a type ordinarily supplied for private use or consumption. *R & B Customs Brokers* provides an example. A company bought a car but did nevertheless deal as a consumer because it satisfied all three parts of the test which apply to companies. If what the company had bought had been an industrial drilling machine then the company would not have dealt as a consumer. An industrial drilling machine is not a type of goods ordinarily supplied for private use or consumption.

Effect of dealing as a consumer

If a buyer does deal as a consumer then the terms implied by ss.13–15 SGA cannot be excluded or restricted by any contract term. (UCTA 1977 ss.6 and 7). The same is true of the equivalent terms implied by SGITA 1973 and SGSA 1982.

If a buyer does not deal as a consumer then the terms implied by SGA ss.13–15 can be excluded or restricted only in so far as the term which excludes them satisfies the UCTA requirement of reasonableness. The same is true of the equivalent terms implied by SGITA 1973 and SGSA 1982. Section 11(1) UCTA provides that the requirement of reasonableness in relation to a contract term is "that the term shall have been a fair and reasonable one to be included having regard to the circumstances which were, or ought reasonably to have been, known to or in the contemplation of the parties when the contract was made". Section 11(5) provides that the burden of proof is on the party claiming that a contract term or notice does satisfy the requirement of reasonableness to show that it does. Schedule 2 provides five guidelines guidelines to be used when applying the reasonableness test. Regard should be had to any of these guidelines which appear relevant. The matters are:

(a) the strength of the bargaining position of the parties relative to each other, taking into account (among other things) alternative means by which the customer's requirements could have been met;

(b) Whether the customer received an inducement to agree to the term, or in accepting it had an opportunity of entering into a similar contract with other persons, but without having to accept a similar term;

(c) Whether the customer knew or ought reasonably to have known of the existence and extent of the term (having regard, among other things, to any custom of the trade and any previous course of dealing between the parties);

(d) where the term excludes or restricts any relevant liability if some condition is not complied with, whether it was reasonable at the time of the contract to expect that compliance with the term would be practicable;

(e) whether the goods were manufactured, processed or adapted to the special order of the customer.

Exclusion of the terms implied into contracts to provide a service

We have already seen that ss.14 and 15 SGSA are subject to contrary agreement. So s.14 fixes a time for the performance of the service only if no time was expressly or impliedly agreed. Similarly, s.15 implies that a reasonable price will be paid only if no price has been fixed.

As regards s.13 SGSA, we saw that the requirement to provide the service using reasonable care and skill imposes a tort standard. Section 1 UCTA 1977 tells us that breach of this term is regarded as "negligence" for the purposes of UCTA 1977. Consequently, exclusion of this term is governed by s.2 UCTA. Section 2(1) UCTA provides that no contract term or notice can allow a person to exclude liability for death or personal injury resulting from negligence.Section 2(2) allows the exclusion of other loss or damage caused by negligence only in so far as the term or notice which does this satisfies the UCTA requirement of reasonableness. The following figure shows the extent to which UCTA 1977 allows the statutory implied terms to be excluded.

THE UNFAIR TERMS IN CONSUMER CONTRACTS REGU-LATIONS 1999

To which contracts do the Regs apply?

These Regs, which run alongside UCTA 1977, apply to unfair terms in contracts between a seller or supplier and a consumer. (Regulation 4(1).) They apply whether the contract was to supply either goods or services, and do not specifically deal with exclusion of statutory implied terms. They can however render ineffective terms which try to exclude liability for breach of the statutory implied terms.

The definition of a consumer is **not the same** as the definition in UCTA. Here a consumer is defined as a natural person who is acting for purposes outside his trade, business or profession. (Regulation 3(1).) So a company cannot be a consumer for the purposes of the Regs. Anyone, either a company or an individual, who is acting for purposes relating to his business, trade or profession is regarded as a seller or supplier. (Regulation 3(1).)

Figure 2.2

Can the implied terms be excluded

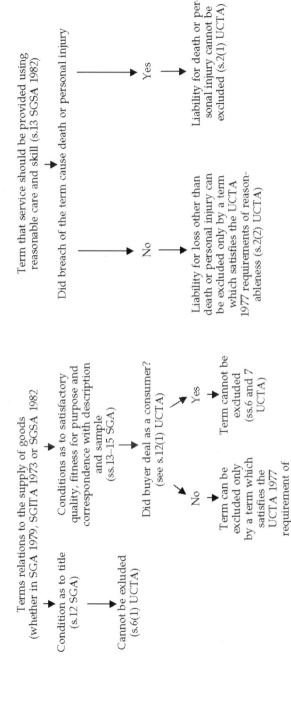

When is a term unfair?

Regulation 5(1) provides that a contractual term which has not been individually negotiated shall be regarded as unfair if, contrary to the requirement of good faith, it causes a significant imbalance in the parties' rights and obligations, arising under the contract, to the detriment of the consumer.

There are several points to note about this definition. First, a term which was individually negotiated with the consumer will not be regarded as unfair. Second, a term can be regarded as unfair only if it is **contrary to the requirement of good faith**. This requirement is not spelt out, but in assessing it the court will consider all of the relevant circumstances. Third, the term must cause a **significant imbalance in the parties' rights and obligations, to the detriment of the consumer**. In *Director-General of Fair Trading v First National Bank* [2001] Lord Bingham said that "the requirement of significant imbalance is met if a term is so weighted in favour of the supplier as to tilt the parties' rights and obligations under the contract significantly in his favour." He said that good faith, on the other hand required fair and open dealing, so that there were no hidden traps. It also required that terms which were disadvantageous to the consumer should be given prominence and that the supplier should not take advantage of the consumer's disadvantageous position.

Schedule 2 of the Regs sets out a "grey list" which gives examples of terms which may be regarded as unfair. This list is not exhaustive, so a term will not automatically be fair just because it does not resemble any term in the grey list.

Terms which are written in plain, intelligible English and which set out what is being bought, and the price for which it is being bought, will not be regarded as unfair. So the Regs are not attempting to make sure that a consumer's consideration is worth much the same as that of the seller or supplier.

Effect of a term being unfair

If a term is regarded by the Regs as unfair then that particular term shall not be binding on the consumer. (Regulation 8(1).) However, the rest of the contract stands if it is capable of continuing in existence without the unfair term. (Regulation 8(2).)

Reform of UCTA and the Regs

The Law Commission has proposed that UCTA 1977 and the 1999 Regs should be merged into one new statute. This will not be easy, as they adopt fundamentally different approaches to dealing with exclusion clauses.

---

3. THE TRANSFER OF PROPERTY: RISK, MISTAKE AND FRUSTRATION

Overview

Under a contract of sale of goods the property in the goods (ownership of the goods) is passed from the seller to the buyer. The Sale of Goods Act sets out definite rules on the precise time at which property passes. These rules vary, depending upon whether the goods sold were specific or unascertained. The Act also sets out the circumstances in which contracts for the sale of specific goods can be frustrated or void for mistake. Before we consider the provisions of the Act in more detail, we first need to know why it can be important to decide exactly when the property passes from seller to buyer.

Reasons for wanting to know whether the property has passed

There are two main reasons for wanting to know whether or not the property has passed from the seller to the buyer.

The first reason is that s.20(1) provides that **the risk** will pass with the property unless the parties have agreed otherwise. The party who has the risk takes the risk of the goods being damaged or destroyed. (Risk is dealt with in more detail later in this chapter on p.46.)

Example

On Monday Sarah made a contract to sell her car to Billy. If the car was damaged **before** the property had passed to Billy then the car would have been at Sarah's risk when damaged. Billy could therefore reject the car, for breach of the implied term as to satisfactory quality, and claim damages. Furthermore, if the price had not yet been paid, Billy would have no obligation to pay it, and if the price had been paid Billy could reclaim it. If the car was damaged **after** the property and risk had passed to Billy then he would have no claim against Sarah regarding the damage and would have to pay the price, if it had not already been paid.

The second reason for wanting to know whether or not property has passed is that either the buyer or the seller might have become **insolvent**. (The risk is not concerned with the risk of the other party becoming insolvent, it is concerned only with the risk of the goods being damaged or destroyed by a person other than the buyer or the seller.)

Let us first consider the position where **the seller has become insolvent**. If the property in the goods had passed to the buyer before the seller became insolvent then the buyer would own the goods, even if he had not yet got possession of them. The buyer would of course have to pay the full price to the seller's liquidator, if this had not already been paid to the seller. But the buyer would be entitled to delivery of the goods. If the seller became insolvent before the property had passed to the buyer then the buyer would not have become the owner of the goods. The buyer would therefore have to return the goods if they had already been delivered to him and, if they had not been delivered, would have no right to demand delivery. If the buyer had paid the price, he would have the right to reclaim this on the grounds that there had been a total failure of consideration. However, such a claim would have to be made against the liquidator. As the buyer would merely be an unsecured creditor, it is unlikely that the he would receive the return of much of the money paid. (See retention of title, later in this chapter, where the position of unsecured creditors claiming against liquidators is set out.)

Now let us consider the position where it is **the buyer who has become insolvent**. If the property had passed to the buyer before he became insolvent then the seller would not be able to reclaim the goods as he no would no longer own them. If the buyer had paid the full price then the seller would not be disadvantaged. But if the buyer had not yet paid the price the seller could claim for the price only as an unsecured creditor against the buyer's liquidator. If the property had not passed to the buyer at the time of his insolvency then the seller would still own the goods and could therefore keep, or recover, possession of them. However, the buyer's liquidator could enforce the contract by paying the full price. If the liquidator did not do this, the seller would have to hand over to the liquidator any part of the price which the buyer had already paid, as there would have been a total failure of consideration.

The transfer of property in specific goods

In Ch.1, on p.4, we distinguished specific and unascertained goods. When considering the transfer of property this distinction is absolutely vital. **You must always begin by deciding whether the goods are specific or unascertained** because if they are specific you follow one set or rules, whereas if they are unascertained you follow a completely different set of rules.

You should remember that s.61(1) defines specific goods as goods which were identified and agreed upon at the time when the contract of sale was made. This means identified and agreed upon by both the buyer and the seller, so that both parties know exactly which goods are being sold. You should also remember that unascertained goods include any goods which are not specific. Such goods are sold merely by description.

Example

Brendan phones a paint dealer and contracts to buy 10 tins of white gloss paint. The goods are not specific because they have not been identified and agreed upon by both parties. The contract is therefore for the sale of unascertained goods and the dealer could perform the contract by delivering any 10 tins of paint which matched the contract description. Brendan then asks the dealer whether a second-hand paint-mixing machine, which he saw in the shop yesterday, is still for sale. The dealer says that it is and Brendan buys it. The contract is for the sale of specific goods because both parties have identified and agreed upon the goods which are being sold. The seller could not therefore perform the contract by delivering any other goods.

Once it has been decided that goods are specific, ss.17 and 18 are applied, **in that order. Section 17 provides that the property in specific goods will pass when the parties intended it to pass.** Section 18 sets out four rules to be applied to specific goods, in the event that the parties did not make their intentions clear. So if s.17 applies we do not need to consider s.18. The four s.18 rules are now considered in turn.

Section 18 Rule 1—specific goods in a deliverable state

Rule 1 provides that where there is an unconditional sale of specific goods in a deliverable state the property in the goods passes to the buyer when the contract is made, even if payment or delivery are made afterwards. This clearly demonstrates that the passing of the property is not connected to possession of the property. *Tarling v Baxter (1827)* provides an example of Rule 1. A haystack was sold on January 6. The terms of the contract provided that the buyer was to pay the price on 4 February and that the haystack would not be moved before May 1. The haystack was destroyed by fire on January 20. As the sale was of specific goods in a deliverable state, the property had passed to the buyer on January 6.

Section 18 Rule 2—specific goods which the seller has to put into a deliverable state

Rule 2 provides that where specific goods are sold and the seller is bound to do something to the goods for the purpose of putting them into a deliverable state, the property does not pass until the thing has been done and the buyer has notice that it has been done. In *Underwood Ltd v Burgh CBCS (1922)* a 30 ton condensing engine was sold on February 20. The contract provided that the seller should detach the engine from its concrete bed and put it "free on rail". The engine was damaged whilst the engine was being loaded onto the train. Section 17 applied and property had not passed because the engine had not yet been put "free on rail". Alternatively, Rule 2 applied and the property had not passed to the buyer because the seller had not done what he had agreed to do to the goods and had not also informed the buyer that this had been done.

Point of uncertainty

The crucial difference between Rules 1 and 2 is that Rule 1 applies if the goods were in a deliverable state at the time of the contract, whereas Rule 2 applies if the seller was bound to do something to the goods to put them into a deliverable state. There is surprisingly little authority on the meaning of "in a deliverable state". In *Underwood Ltd v Burgh CBCS* Rowlatt J. said that the fact that goods needed to be packaged or dismantled prior to delivery would not prevent them from being in a deliverable state. Goods would be in a deliverable state, he said, when they were in the state in which they were the thing which the buyer had contracted to buy. The key test was whether or not the seller yet had an obligation to do anything to the goods, as an article, to put them into such a state.

Figure 3.1

The passing of Property in Specific Goods

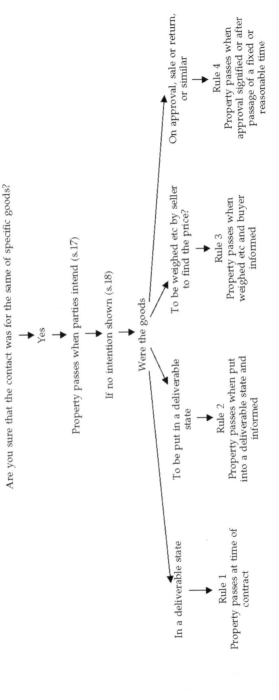

Are you sure that the contact was for the same of specific goods?

→ Yes →

Property passes when parties intend (s.17)

If no intention shown (s.18)

Were the goods

In a deliverable state
Rule 1
Property passes at time of contract

To be put in a deliverable state
Rule 2
Property passes when put into a deliverable state and informed

To be weighed etc by seller to find the price?
Rule 3
Property passes when weighed etc and buyer informed

On approval, sale or return, or similar
Rule 4
Property passes when approval signified or after passage of a fixed or reasonable time

Section 18 Rule 3—specific goods which have to be weighed, measured or tested by the seller in order to find the price.

Rule 3 is straightforward. It applies when the seller has to weigh, measure, or test specific goods, or do some other act, in order to find out the price. Property passes only when the goods have been weighed etc and the buyer has been informed of this. Notice that the goods must be specific, that they must be in a deliverable state and that the weighing etc must be done by the seller and in order to find the price.

Section 18 Rule 4—specific goods sold on approval or sale or return

Rule 4 applies where goods are delivered to the buyer on approval, or on sale or return, or on other similar terms. It states that the property passes: (a) when the buyer signifies his approval to the seller or does any act adopting the transaction (such as re-selling the goods or consuming them); or (b) when the buyer keeps the goods for longer than the time fixed in the contract or, if no time was fixed, keeps the goods for more than a reasonable time.

THE TRANSFER OF PROPERTY IN UNASCERTAINED GOODS

Sections 16, 17 and 18 Rule 5 govern the passing of the property in unascertained goods. **These sections must be applied in that order**. First s.16 is applied, then s.17 is applied and then, if necessary, s.18 Rule 5 is applied.

Section 16 provides that property in unascertained goods **cannot pass** (subject to s.20A) until the goods are ascertained. So it does not tell us when property will pass, it merely tells us when property cannot pass. Goods become ascertained when they are identified as the goods to be used to perform the contract. (*Re Wait* [1927].) Once goods have become ascertained they bear some similarity to specific goods. However, **unascertained goods never become specific goods.** If the contract was for the sale of unascertained goods you apply ss.16, 17 and 18 Rule 5. You do not apply s.18 Rules 1—4.

Once the goods are ascertained, s.17 provides that the property will pass when the parties intended it to. If the intentions of the parties cannot be found, then the rule of presumed intention in s.18 Rule 5 will apply. Rule 5 states that the property will pass when goods matching the contract description and in a deliverable state are unconditionally appropriated to the contract with the assent of the other party. We have already considered the meaning of "in a deliverable state" in relation to s.18 Rules 1 and 2. Goods are unconditionally appropriated to the contract when the goods are irrevocably earmarked as the particular goods to be used to perform the contract. (*Carlos Federspiel & Co v Charles Twigg & Co Ltd* [1957].) If the unconditional appropriation is performed by the seller then the buyer must assent to it. If it is done by the buyer (which would be unusual) the seller must assent to it. This assent may be express but is more often implied. Once the unconditional appropriation has been assented to and performed then the seller cannot change his mind and use substitute goods. The goods which have been unconditionally appropriated will now belong to the buyer as this is what the buyer and the seller are presumed to have intended. Often the goods are ascertained and unconditionally appropriated at the same time.

Appropriation by delivery to a carrier

Section 18 Rule 5(2) says that if the seller delivers the goods to a carrier for the purpose of transmission to the buyer, in pursuance of the contract, this is regarded as an unconditional appropriation of the goods. There are several points to note. First, this will not be an unconditional appropriation if the goods have not been ascertained. (*Healy v Howlett & Sons* [1917].) For example, if one bulk of goods is delivered to the carrier for transmission to two different buyers, property will not pass to either buyer as the goods have not become ascertained. Second, the carrier must not be the seller's agent. Third, the section will not apply if the seller reserves title in the goods. Reservation of title is considered later in this chapter. Section 18 Rule 5(2), being part of s.18, is subject to contrary intention.

Appropriation by exhaustion

Section 18 Rule 5(3) provides that in certain circumstances the goods can be unconditionally appropriated by exhaustion, causing property in them to pass to the buyer. The following conditions must **all** be fulfilled. First, there must have been a sale of a specified quantity of unascertained goods forming part of a bulk. Second, this bulk must have been identified either by the contract or by subsequent agreement between the parties. Third, the bulk must have been reduced to the amount of goods due to the buyer, or to less than this amount. Finally, the buyer must be the only buyer to whom goods are then due out of the bulk. If all of these conditions are satisfied then the goods which remain in the bulk are appropriated to the buyer and he becomes the owner of these goods. (When the bulk was reduced to the amount due to the final buyer, that buyer's goods would also have been ascertained.) A "bulk" is defined by s.61(1) as a mass or collection of goods of the same kind which (a) is contained in a defined space or area and (b) is such that any of the goods in the bulk are interchangeable with any other goods therein of the same number or quantity. Section 18 Rule 5(3), being part of s.18, is subject to contrary intention.

Example

S tells X, Y and Z that he wants to sell a consignment of 50 tons of wheat which is stored in a certain warehouse. X and Y both agree to buy 20 tons of this wheat and Z agrees to buy 10 tons of it. S removes 20 tons and delivers it to X. S then removes another 20 tons and delivers it to Y. As soon as the bulk is reduced to just 10 tons, the property in these 10 tons passes to Z under s.18 Rule 5(3).

UNDIVIDED SHARES IN GOODS FORMING PART OF A BULK

Section 20A allows a buyer of unascertained goods which form part of a bulk to become a co-owner of the bulk if four conditions, set out in s.20A(1), are **all** satisfied. The conditions are as follows.

First, a specified quantity of unascertained goods must have been bought. Second, the goods must form part of a bulk. Third, the bulk must have been identified in the contract or by subsequent agreement between the parties. Fourth, the buyer must have paid some or all of the price. If any of these conditions are not satisfied then s.20A will not apply.

If all of the conditions are satisfied the buyer becomes an owner in common of the whole bulk, unless the parties agree otherwise. (Section 20A(2).) The extent of the buyer's co-ownership **at any time** is calculated by dividing the quantity

of goods which the buyer **has paid for**, and which are due to
the buyer, by the quantity of goods in the bulk at the appropriate time. (Section 20A(3).)

Example

S tells B that he has 10 tons of oats stored on a certain ship and
that B can buy any or all of these oats at £100 a ton. B buys 4
tons and pays £400. All of the conditions set out in s.20A(1) are
satisfied and so B becomes an owner in common of the whole 10
tons. (Section 20A(2).) B is a 4/10 (or 2/5) co-owner because he
has paid for 4 tons and the bulk is 10 tons. (Section 20A(3).) If B
had agreed to buy 4 tons but had paid for only 2 tons he would
be a 2/10 (or 1/5) co-owner. (Section 20A(3).) When B collects
his 4 tons he will become owner of those 4 tons (by virtue of
ss.16, 17 and 18 Rule 5) and will cease to be a co-owner of the
remaining bulk. If B is a 4/10 co-owner of the bulk of 10 tons
and the bulk is reduced to 5 tons then B becomes a 4/5 co-
owner of the remaining 5 tons. (Section 20A(3).) The size of the
bulk has been reduced, but the quantity of goods which should
ultimately be delivered to B has not.

If more goods are sold than are in the bulk, the undivided
shares of each of the buyers is reduced proportionately. (Section
20A(4).)

Example

S has 8 tons of wheat in a certain warehouse and sells some of
this wheat to two buyers, A and B, in such a way that the
conditions set out in s.20A are satisfied. By mistake, S sells 8
tons to A and 4 tons to B. The buyers in common are due,
between them, 12 tons but the bulk contains only 8 tons. The
share of A and B is reduced proportionately. So A is a 2/3
owner in common of the bulk of 8 tons and B is a 1/3 owner in
common. (Both A and B can pursue their usual remedies if they
do not receive the quantity contracted for.)

If a buyer has paid only some of the price for goods due to
him out of a bulk, any delivery of goods to that buyer from the
bulk is regarded first as the goods the buyer has paid for.
(Section 20A(5).)

Deemed consent by co-owner to dealing in bulk goods

Section 20B(1)(a) says that a buyer who becomes a co-owner of a
bulk under s.20A(1) is deemed to consent to any delivery out of

the bulk to any other owner in common out of the bulk if the goods delivered are due to that buyer under his contract. Section 20B(1)(b) provides that co-owners by virtue of s.20A are also deemed to consent to any removal or delivery of the goods by any other co-owner (including the seller) as long as the removal or delivery falls within that co-owner's share of the bulk. These provisions are necessary because otherwise all of the buyer co-owners could refuse to allow delivery of any of the goods on the grounds that they were co-owners of the whole bulk. If goods are delivered to a buyer who is a co-owner under s.20A, and this causes a shortfall in the bulk so that there are not enough goods for all the other buyers, the buyer who received the delivery has no obligation to compensate any of the other buyers. (Section 20B(3)(a).)

At whose risk is the bulk?

Sections 20A and B were introduced into the SGA in 1995 to protect buyers of unascertained goods, forming part of an identified bulk, from the insolvency of the seller. The sections effectively do this. If we go back to the first example, where S sold 4 tons of oats to B, we can see how this has been achieved. Before the amendments were introduced, B could not have had any ownership of any of the oats as he had bought unascertained goods. Section 16 would have defeated him. So if S became insolvent B would merely be an unsecured creditor who would not be able to get much, if any, of his £400 back. After the amendments B has become a 2/5 co-owner of the whole bulk. (Section 16 is now expressly stated to be subject to s.20A.) The easiest way for S's liquidator to deal with this situation will be to deliver 4 tons of the oats to B, who is thus protected.

The new provisions do not expressly deal with the risk. On the one hand it might be thought that the risk would be shared equally amongst all of the co-owners, as s.20(1) provides that unless otherwise agreed the risk passes with the property. However, ss.20A(3) suggests otherwise. By stating that the undivided share of a buyer in a bulk at any time is calculated by dividing the quantity of goods which that buyer has paid for by the quantity of goods in the bulk, this suggests that any loss of the goods is first borne by the seller. Also, s.20B(3)c) states that nothing in s.20A affects the rights of a buyer under his contract. So the position as regards the risk is not clear.

RISK

Risk means the risk of theft, or of damage to the goods, or of destruction of the goods. It does not mean the risk of a party becoming insolvent. The party who has the risk will be obliged to perform the contract, despite the damage etc. So if specific goods are destroyed whist at the seller's risk, the seller will be liable for failure to deliver the goods. If unascertained goods which the seller intended to use to perform the contract were destroyed whilst at the seller's risk, the seller would have to deliver alternative goods which matched the contract description, or will be liable for failure to deliver the goods. If goods were destroyed whilst at the buyer's risk the buyer could not claim non-delivery and would have to pay the price.

Section 20(1) provides that, unless the parties agree otherwise, the risk is transferred at the same time as the property in the goods, whether delivery has been made or not.

Example

Under separate contracts, P sells to Q a second-hand car and 20 gallons of petrol. The parties show no intention as to when the property or the risk should pass. Before the car is delivered or the petrol ascertained, both are destroyed by fire. The risk in the car will have been with Q because property would have passed to Q under s.18 Rule 1. Q will therefore have to pay the full price of the car even though he never got possession of it. The risk in the petrol will have been with P because property would not have passed to Q (s.16). So Q will have to deliver 20 gallons of petrol matching the contract description or will be in breach of contract.

If the fault of either the buyer or the seller delays delivery of the goods then the goods are at the risk of the party who caused the delay as regards any loss which might not have occurred but for such fault. (Section 20(2).)

Section 20(3) provides that nothing in s.20 affects the duties or liabilities of the buyer or seller as bailee of the goods. A bailee possesses goods which he does not own. The main duties of a bailee are to deliver the goods, if so requested, and not to negligently damage the goods. Buyers and sellers are commonly bailees of the goods sold. For example, sellers of specific goods in a deliverable state will always be bailees of the goods after the contract is made, unless they immediately deliver the goods. Buyers to whom goods are delivered on sale or return will be bailees of the goods until they either return the goods or cause the property to pass.

Risk whist in transit

Section 32(1) provides that where in pursuance of a contract of sale, the seller is authorised or required to send the goods to the buyer, delivery of the goods to a carrier for the purpose of transmission to the buyer is prima facie deemed to be delivery of the goods to the buyer.

This rule is similar to s.18 Rule 5(2) which was considered earlier in this chapter. It means that the risk will pass to the buyer when the goods are delivered to a carrier. But the rule will not apply if the goods delivered to the carrier have not yet been ascertained. As with s.18 Rule 5(2), the carrier must be an independent carrier and must not be the agent of the seller. Nor does the section apply if the contract has specified a particular place as being the place of delivery.

If the seller does make the contract of carriage on behalf of the buyer then he must make a reasonable contract, having regard to the nature of the goods and all the circumstances of the case. If the seller fails to do this, and the goods are lost or damaged in the course of transit, the buyer can either regard the goods as not having been delivered or can sue the seller for damages (Section 32(2).)

Section 32(3) provides that where the seller agrees to deliver the goods at his own risk to a place other than the place where they were sold, the buyer must take any risk of deterioration of the goods which is necessarily incident to the contract of transport. This section is subject to contrary intention. Furthermore, it applies only to a risk of deterioration which is **necessarily incident** to the contract of transport.

Mistake and frustration

The common law can hold a contract void for mistake if the contract was impossible to perform when it was made. It can also hold a contract frustrated if the contract subsequently becomes illegal to perform, impossible to perform or radically different from what the parties contemplated when they made the contract. When a contract is frustrated at common law, the

Law Reform (Frustrated Contracts) Act 1943 sets out the legal effects. (See *Nutshell on Contract*.)

Sections 6 and 7 SGA make special rules about mistake and frustration but these rules **can apply only to contracts for the sale of specific goods**. Future goods (see definitions in Ch.1) are always regarded as unascertained, when applying the SGA rules on the transfer of property. However, **it is probably the case** that future goods can, if they are already physically in existence, be regarded as specific for the purposes of ss.6 and 7.

Section 6 provides that where there is a contract for the sale of specific goods, and the goods without the knowledge of the seller have perished at the time the contract is made, the contract is void.

Section 7 provides that where there is an agreement to sell specific goods and subsequently the goods, without any fault on the part of the seller or the buyer, perish before the risk passes to the buyer the contract is avoided. (The LRFCA 1943 does not apply when s.7 SGA does apply.)

Example

On January 20, X agrees to sell his second-hand car to Y. If unknown to X the car had been destroyed by fire on January 19, s.6 would hold the contract void. Therefore, X would not be in breach of contract when he failed to deliver the car, and any money paid by Y would have to be refunded. If the car was destroyed on January 21 then the contract would **not** be frustrated. Risk and property would have passed to Y when the contract was made. (Sections18 Rule 1 and 20(1).) But if a term of the contract had provided that property in the car should not pass to Y until January 22, and the car had been destroyed on January 21, then the contract would be frustrated under s.7. X would therefore not be in breach of contract and Y could reclaim any money already paid.

We have seen that ss.6 and 7 can apply only to contracts for the sale of specific goods. Furthermore, they apply only if the goods **perished**. Goods which have been destroyed have obviously perished. Goods will also have perished if they become so altered that for business purposes they can no longer be said to be the goods sold. For example, in *Asfar v Blundell* [1896] a cargo of dates which had sunk in the Thames and became covered in sewage was held to have perished. The dates were raised up and could have been distilled into alcohol but would not be regarded by businessmen as still being dates. In *Barrow, Lane and Ballard Ltd v Phillip Phillips & Co Ltd* [1929] it was held that a consignment of goods had perished because a significant part of them had been stolen. However, the court accepted that there was no prospect at all of the stolen goods being recovered. This case must therefore be applied with caution. If there is a good prospect of recovery, as there usually is when a car is stolen, the goods may well not be regarded as having perished.

Section 6 will not apply if the seller guarantees that the goods exist or if the seller knows that the goods do not exist at the time of the contract. Section 7 will not apply if it is the fault of the buyer or the seller that the goods perish. There is some dispute as to whether or not s.7 is subject to a contrary intention being shown by the parties. It seems likely that s.7 will not apply if a term of the contract provides either that the seller guarantees that the goods will not perish, or that the buyer will bear the consequences if the goods do perish.

RETENTION OF TITLE

A retention of title clause can enable a seller to deliver goods to a buyer on terms that the buyer will not become the owner of the goods until the full price has been paid.

As we have seen, s.17(1) SGA provides that the property in goods will pass from seller to buyer when the parties intend that it should. Section 19(1) goes further and expressly provides that the seller may reserve title until certain conditions are fulfilled. Sections 17(1) and 19(1) therefore allow simple reservation of title clauses to be effective. However, to be effective, a retention of title clause **must be incorporated** into the contract between buyer and seller. The incorporation of contractual terms is considered in *Nutshell on Contract*. Briefly, a retention of title clause will be incorporated if it is agreed between the parties, either expressly or impliedly. Such clauses are often impliedly incorporated by a regular course of dealing between the parties.

A reservation of title clause is likely to be invoked where a **buyer becomes insolvent** before paying the full price of goods. A seller who makes a claim for the price will be an **unsecured creditor** of the buyer. Such unsecured creditors are paid after preferential creditors and secured creditors. (Although recent changes to insolvency law set aside a small pot of money which is top-sliced for unsecured creditors.) When a business becomes insolvent unsecured creditors will not be paid all that they are owed, and are often paid a very small percentage of what they are owed. If a seller has supplied goods to an insolvent buyer and the contract contained an effective retention of title clause then the seller **will be able to retake the goods** from the buyer's liquidator. This is because ownership of the goods never passed to the buyer but remained with the seller all the time.

Example

Manufacture Ltd sells and delivers 100 sofas to Retail Ltd. A term of the contract provides that ownership of the goods is not to pass until the full price has been paid. The next week Retail Ltd becomes insolvent with massive debts. None of the contract price has yet been paid. Manufacture Ltd can go and collect their 100 sofas because ownership of these sofas never passed to Retail Ltd. If Manufacture Ltd did not have an effective retention of title clause then property in the sofas would have passed to Retail Ltd by the time the sofas were delivered. Consequently, a claim for the price by Manufacture Ltd would merely be made as an unsecured creditor of Retail Ltd. As Retail Ltd has massive debts, Manufacture Ltd would, at best, receive only a small percentage of the price it was owed.

The retention of title clause in the example above is known as a simple reservation of title clause. It does not attempt to gain any security other than by means of providing that the property in the particular goods sold will not pass until payment has been made. Such clauses are effective (*Clough Mill Ltd v Martin* [1984]). When clauses attempt to gain more extensive security then difficulties can arise. Before we examine these difficulties we should consider difficulties which can arise even in relation to a simple retention of title clause.

Goods resold by the buyer

If the goods are resold by a buyer who bought them subject to a retention of title clause, then s.25 SGA provides that the sub-buyer gets good title to the goods as long as he acted in good faith and without knowing of the retention of title clause. The ROT clause will be ineffective against the sub-buyer, who will gain ownership of the goods. (Section 25 is considered in Ch.4 under the heading "Buyer in possession".) So, to extend the example above, if Retail Ltd had sold some or all of the sofas to members of the public then Manufacture Ltd would not have been allowed to retake these sofas from those members of the public, even if the retention of title clause said that it could.

Goods must be identifiable

A retention of title clause allows a seller to reserve title to the goods sold. If the goods sold become so changed that they lose their identity then the seller will not be able to reclaim them. If the goods are merely mixed with other identical goods then it seems likely that a seller with an ROT clause will be an owner in common of the whole mixture. In *Indian Oil Corp Ltd v Greenstone Shipping* [1988] oil was sold subject to a ROT clause. This oil was put into the hold of a ship where it became mixed with someone else's oil. The seller was held to be an owner in common of all the oil in the hold, so that he could recover the quantity of oil which he had sold.

Unregistered charges

If a company gives a property interest as security for a debt then this is regarded as the granting of a charge. If such a charge is not registered with Companies House within 21 days of creation then the security which the charge provided will be lost. (Companies Act 1985 ss.395 and 396.) If the charge is properly registered then the chargeholder ranks high up if the company becomes insolvent. A **fixed charge** is taken over certain identifiable assets and is a mortgage over those assets. So if the company which granted the charge becomes insolvent the holder of a fixed charge can sell those assets charged and take from the proceeds of sale what he is owed, ahead of any other creditors of the insolvent company. A **floating charge** is taken over a class of assets as a whole, rather than over any identified assets. A floating chargeholder is a "secured creditor" and although not the first to be paid out of the assets which the company liquidator gathers in, ranks above unsecured creditors. (If the charge was created after September 15, 2003 a small amount is 'top-sliced' for unsecured creditors. However, charge holders are still in a much better position than unsecured creditors.)

Example

A Ltd goes into insolvent liquidation. B is owed £10,000 and has taken a fixed charge over A Ltd's delivery lorry as security for this amount. C is owed £500,000 and has taken a floating charge over all of A Ltd's other assets as security. Unsecured creditors are owed £1 million. B can sell the delivery lorry and take £10,000 from the proceeds, ahead of any other creditor. (Any surplus goes into the pool of assets.) The other assets of A Ltd will be sold and C will take the £500,000 he is owed from the proceeds, ahead of debts being paid to unsecured creditors. (Subject to possible "top-slicing".)

It has been argued that certain types of ROT clauses are in fact charges. If this is true of any ROT clause then it will be invalid as an unregistered charge. Slade J. in *Re Bond Worth* said that any contract will be a charge if it creates an interest in property to secure a debt, and if that interest will cease to exist if the debt is repaid. We will see that several types of ROT clauses would probably amount to charges if this view is correct. The obvious answer to this problem might seem to be for the seller to register his ROT clause as a charge. However, it would be impractical to do this every time goods were sold, and besides any charge so registered would rank behind other charges which had already been registered.

Goods which have entered the manufacturing process

Once goods sold subject to an ROT clause have been manufactured into other goods, then a simple ROT clause will be no good if the goods sold have ceased to exist. (*Borden (UK) Ltd v Scottish Timber Products Ltd* [1981].) To combat this, an ROT clause might go further and claim to give the seller ownership of the manufactured goods until the original goods sold have been paid for. In *Re Peachdart Ltd* [1983] it was held that any claim to the manufactured goods would be void as an unregistered charge. The reasoning was that once the goods sold were manufactured into other goods the parties would have intended that they should cease to belong to the seller. The buyer would then have owned the property. So any interest which the seller might subsequently have gained would be a property interest given to the seller to secure the payment of a debt, that is to say, a charge. This approach was followed in *Modelboard Ltd v Outer Box Ltd* [1993] in which cardboard had lost all value as a raw material once it had been manufactured into cardboard boxes. Also, if value is added the buyer would receive a windfall profit if he became entitled to the goods. The parties would never have intended the buyer to receive such a windfall profit.

If the goods sold are merely altered in some way, without losing their value as raw material, and without any value being added, then there is no reason why the seller's ROT clause should be regarded as a charge. The seller is not being given any additional security by the buyer, he is merely retaining title to the goods sold. For example, in *Armour v Thyssen* steel supplied by the seller was cut into lengths but this did not prevent the seller from reclaiming it, as no value had been added by the buyer.

If the goods sold have merely been attached to other goods, rather than manufactured into new goods, then a seller with a ROT clause may be able to detach the goods sold if this can be done without causing damage. (*Hendy Lennox Ltd v Grahame Puttick Ltd* [1984].) Here the seller will not be making a windfall profit as he will not be gaining any property which ever belonged to the buyer. Therefore no charge will have been created.

All moneys clauses

An all moneys clause goes further than a simple ROT clause. It provides that the buyer of goods will not own the goods until he has paid all money which is owing to the seller. So it would claim that a buyer who had paid for the goods delivered would not own these goods if the buyer still owed the seller money from a previous delivery. Where a buyer and seller deal with each other regularly, and where the buyer is given credit, such clauses could therefore mean that the buyer would never own any of the goods delivered if the buyer never completely cleared his account with the seller. There seems to be a strong argument why such an all moneys clause creates a charge. The buyer is taking as security goods other than those being sold and if the price is paid then the security will cease to exist. But in *Armour v Thyssen Edelstahlwerke AG* [1990] the House of Lords held than an all-moneys clause did not create a charge. However, the decision is somewhat unsatisfactory as it related only to goods which had not been paid for. The court did not consider whether goods which had been paid for earlier could be recovered by the seller. Also, the reasoning in the case is somewhat circular. It proceeded along the lines of the following; because the ROT clause was effective, no property ever passed to the buyer; so the buyer never had any property in the goods to give to the seller as security for the debt; so the ROT was not a charge; and so it was effective.

Clough Mill Ltd v Martin [1984] considered the position where the seller uses a ROT clause to reclaim the actual goods sold under that particular contract, and the goods reclaimed are worth more than the debt which the buyer owes to the seller. The Court of Appeal thought that the seller could do this and that no charge would have been created. Two explanations were put forward. First, the contract remained in force, and the seller could resell the goods and take only what he was owed, returning any surplus to the buyer. Second, the contract had ceased to exist, so the seller could resell the goods and keep all of the proceeds. But then the seller would have committed a total failure of consideration and so he would have to give the buyer all of the purchase price back (less any damages which were due to the seller). Both of these approaches will have much the same effect, the seller will be paid what he is owed and the surplus will go to the buyer. The Court of Appeal held that no charge was created because no title ever passed to the buyer and so he could not confer a charge over the property. (This was the reasoning later adopted by the House of Lords in *Armour v Thyssen*.)

If the seller claims goods other than those sold under the particular contract, (under an all-moneys clause) and these goods are worth more than the amount owed, the seller would make a windfall profit if he kept all the proceeds of sale. *Clough Mill* did not decide whether such a claim might be effective. But since the seller would have been given something as security for a debt, and since this security would cease to exist if the debt was paid, this would seem to be a charge. To counter this, the seller might claim to be due only what he was owed out of the proceeds of sale of the repossessed property with any surplus going to the buyer. If the seller did this he would recognise that he had only a limited interest in this property. This then would again seem to be a charge as the seller would recognise that he did not have complete ownership of the goods, but only a property interest to secure a debt.

Retaining equitable and beneficial ownership

If the seller retains equitable and beneficial ownership, rather than legal ownership, then Slade J. in *Re Bond Worth* [1980] held that both legal ownership and equitable ownership pass to the buyer. The equitable ownership passes for only a fraction of a second. But because the seller is given back equitable ownership he has taken this as security for the payment of a debt. This security will cease to exist if the debt is repaid, and so a charge will have been created.

Claims to proceeds of sale

In the *Romalpa* case [1976] aluminium foil which had been sold subject to a ROT clause was sold on by the buyer. The seller could not reclaim the foil from the sub-buyer. (See s.25 SGA, above.) The ROT clause was a complex one and required the buyer to keep the foil separate from other foil which the buyer possessed. It also said that if the foil was made into other goods then these goods were to be held on the seller's behalf and that if these manufactured goods were sold the proceeds of sale were to be held on behalf of the seller. The buyer went into liquidation. The seller claimed £50,000 worth of the foil which had not been sold on or manufactured into other goods. The buyer had sold £30,000 of the foil and the seller also claimed the proceeds of this sale. The Court of Appeal held that the buyer was entitled to reclaim the foil and to claim the proceeds of sale. So *Romalpa* is an authority which supports the idea that a claim to the proceeds of sale can be effective. However, there are several reasons why future claims to the proceeds of sale will not be effective. First, in *Romalpa* the buyer's liquidator had conceded that a fiduciary relationship existed between the buyer and seller. He also conceded that the buyer held any manufactured goods as a bailee for the seller who was a "fiduciary owner" of them. No liquidator is likely to concede this again. Second, if there really was a fiduciary relationship then all the proceeds of sale should have been paid into a separate bank account. This would have meant that none of it could have been used by the buyers and was not what the parties intended. Third, if there was a fiduciary relationship then the seller should have been entitled to keep all the proceeds of sale, including any profit, and not to just what he was owed. Fourth, if the buyers did hold the foil as the seller's bailees then they should have been prepared to redeliver the foil to the seller. Neither the buyer nor the seller contemplated this happening. Fifth, if the seller was entitled to only the amount he was owed, out of the proceeds of sale, then this would have been a charge, and the parties cannot have intended that the seller was entitled to more than what he was owed. Sixth, if the goods were held in a fiduciary capacity then they should have been kept separate from the buyer's goods.

The decision in Romalpa has not been followed by subsequent courts. In *Pfeiffer GmbH v Arbuthnot Factors* [1988] it was held that a buyer does not usually resell goods as a bailee of the seller from whom he bought them. Even if the buyer did sell them as the seller's fiduciary the seller would be entitled only to the amount owed. Thus a charge would have been created, as the seller would have taken a property interest to secure a debt and this interest would cease to exist once the debt was paid.

In cases where complex ROT clauses have been held to be effective the court tends to have seen the form of the legal language used as more important than the practical effect of the clause. In cases where clauses have not been given effect the court has seemed more concerned with the effect of the clause and the true intentions of the parties.

4. TRANSFER OF OWNERSHIP BY A PERSON WHO IS NOT THE OWNER

The general rule is that a person who is not the owner of goods cannot pass ownership to anyone else. For example, I do not own your car and so I cannot pass ownership of your car to a third party. This rule, which is set out in s.21(1)SGA, is often referred to by its Latin name *nemo dat quod non habet*. (Literally translated as nobody gives what he does not have, and often abbreviated to *nemo dat*.)

Despite the general *nemo dat* rule, there are circumstances in which ownership of goods can be passed by a person who is not the owner. The SGA deals with six exceptions and the Hire Purchase Act 1964 provides a seventh. The following Figure shows the exceptions.

COMMON LAW AGENCY

The second part of this book deals with agency. We shall see that an agent has the power to make a contract on behalf of another person known as the principal. So it is quite common for agents to sell goods which belong not to themselves but to their principals. An everyday example is provided by shop assistants. They do not sell their own goods, they sell the goods of the principals who employ them.

When we examine agency we shall see that an agent can act for a principal only if the agent has **authority** to do so. This authority usually arises because the principal has agreed with the agent that the agent should do what he does. For example, shop assistants have the power to sell their principals' goods because the principals have agreed with the agents that they should have this power. When the principal agrees that the agent should have authority this is known as **actual authority**.

Agents with **apparent authority** will also have the power to make contracts which bind their principals. Apparent authority does not arise by agreement between principal and agent. It is a form of estoppel which arises when the principal represents to a third party that the "agent" has the power to make a contract. Once the principal has made such a representation, he is estopped from denying it as regards a third party who has acted upon it. So if a shop owner told a shop assistant not to sell a

Figure 4.1

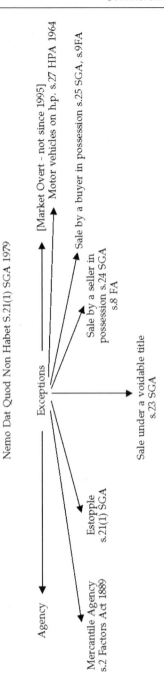

Nemo Dat Quod Non Habet S.21(1) SGA 1979

Exceptions

Agency

Mercantile Agency
s.2 Factors Act 1889

Estopple
s.21(1) SGA

Sale under a voidable title
s.23 SGA

Sale by a seller in
possession s.24 SGA
s.8 FA

[Market Overt - not since 1995]
Motor vehicles on h.p. s.27 HPA 1964

Sale by a buyer in possession s.25 SGA, s.9FA

certain item of stock then the shop assistant would not have actual authority to sell it. However, the shop assistant would have apparent authority to sell it, as long as it was an item which such a shop assistant would usually sell, and a third party who bought the item would be entitled to regard the contract of sale as binding.

If an agent with actual or apparent authority sells the principal's goods then the buyer can enforce the contract and gain ownership of the goods, and there will be no need to consider the other exceptions to the *nemo dat* rule. The wording of s.21(1) SGA, which sets out the *nemo dat* rule, recognises that an agent with authority may pass a good title to the principal's goods. It can be argued that common law agency is not a true exception to the *nemo dat* rule. For example, if I go to a large store and buy goods which a shop assistant has been authorised to sell then all along I know that I am making the contract with the principal rather than with the agent.

MERCANTILE AGENCY (Factors Act 1889 s.2(1))

The requirements of mercantile agency are technical and difficult to establish. So it is important to remember that if a person who might be a mercantile agent has actual or apparent authority to sell the goods then there is no need to consider mercantile agency. Ownership will pass to the buyer on account of the agent having had actual or apparent authority.

The rules relating to mercantile agency are found in the Factors Act 1889. This Act has never been repealed and s.21(2) SGA specifically states that nothing in the SGA affects the provisions of the Factors Act. So it is s.2(1) FA 1889 which provides the definition of a mercantile agent. However, this definition has been refined by many cases. The essential requirements, **all** of which must be satisfied, are as follows.

The mercantile agent must buy or sell goods on behalf of others in a business capacity. However, he might well do this only occasionally, generally buying or selling on his own behalf.

When the mercantile agent sells the goods on to the third party he must possess either the goods themselves or documents of title to the goods.

The possession of the goods or of the documents must have been gained with the owner's consent. This requirement is satisfied even if the owner of the goods was tricked into giving possession to the mercantile agent.

Possession of the goods or the documents must have been given to the mercantile agent in his capacity as a mercantile agent, and so for a purpose connected with sale. This requirement would not be satisfied if the mercantile agent were given goods merely so that he could repair them. But if he were given the goods and asked to invite offers for them it would be satisfied.

The agent must sell or otherwise dispose of the goods. However, an agreement to sell will not do. (The difference between a sale and an agreement to sell was explained in Ch.1.) Furthermore, the sale or disposition must be made in the ordinary course of business of a mercantile agent. This means in business hours, from business premises and in other ways acting as the third party would expect a mercantile agent to be acting. (*Oppenheimer v Attenborough & Son* [1908].)

The third party must take the goods in good faith and without knowing that the mercantile agent had no authority to sell them. The burden of proof is on the third party. (*Heap v Motorist's Advisory Agency Ltd* [1923].)

In all of the exceptions to the *nemo dat* rule, the third party can benefit only if he acted in good faith and without notice of the true owner's rights. Section 61(3) SGA makes it plain that the test of good faith is a subjective one. Notice of the true owner's rights means actual notice. So the third party will gain title as long as he can prove that he had no actual notice of the true owner's rights and also that he considered himself to be acting in good faith. Mere suspicious circumstances will not therefore defeat the third party. However, if the circumstances are so suspicious that a court would think that the third party did not act in good faith and without notice then title will not pass to the third party. For example, in *Heap v Motorist's Advisory Agency Ltd* [1923] a third party bought a car from a rogue for £110, a very low price. The rogue, who was assumed to have acted as a mercantile agent, had bought it for £220. One of the reasons why the third party did not gain title to the car was that he could not prove that he had acted in good faith and without notice of rogue's lack of authority.

Remember! **You must be able to satisfy all of the requirements** of mercantile agency or s.2(1) FA will not allow a non-owner of goods to pass title.

Example

Oswald leaves a watch at Mick's jewellery shop. Oswald asks Mick to sell the watch but to get at least £1,000 for it. Mick agrees to this because he occasionally sells watches for customers. Mick forgets his instructions and sells the watch to Tina for £800. Mick had no actual or apparent authority to sell the watch for £800. (If he had had then Tina could have regarded the contract as binding without the need to prove mercantile agency.) As the requirements of s.2(1) Factors Act were fulfilled Tina becomes owner of the watch. (Oswald could sue Martin for damages for failure to obey his instructions.)

The title which a mercantile agent will pass is the title of the person who consented to him having possession of the goods or the documents. If the person who consented to the mercantile agent having possession was not the owner, (perhaps a thief,) then the mercantile agent will not be able to pass title to the third party.

ESTOPPEL (SGA s.21(1))

The wording of s.21(1) allows for estoppel. Estoppel works in three stages. First, the owner of the goods must represent to a third party that someone else is either the owner of the goods or has the right to sell the goods. Second, the third party must rely on this representation. The consequence of the first two steps is that the owner of the goods is estopped (prevented) from denying the truth of his representation. The third party therefore becomes the owner of the goods.

Merely giving a third party possession of goods is not enough to amount to a representation that the third party is the owner or has the right to sell. (*Jerome v Bentley & Co* [1952].)

Generally, estoppel by negligence will not arise. (*Central Newbury Auctions Ltd v Unity Finance Ltd* [1957].) When a car is let on hire-purchase it is usual for the Finance Company which owns the car to register the cars with HPI. This is so that other dealers can check the HPI register and see that the car is subject to a finance agreement. If a finance company fails to register a car let on hire-purchase with HPI, and another dealer checks the HPI register and buys the car because nothing has been registered, then it might be thought that the finance company had made a representation that the car was free from any financial agreement which should have been registered. The finance company which let the car on hire-purchase might therefore seem to be estopped from claiming the car back from a dealer who checked the HPI register and then bought the car from the hire-purchaser.

However in *Moorgate Mercantile v Twitchings* [1977] the House of Lords rejected such an argument by a bare majority of 3:2.

The person who is not the owner, but who has been represented as the owner, must sell the goods to the third party. An agreement to sell will not do. (*Shaw v Metropolitan Police Commissioner* [1987].)

The title which is passed is only the title which the person who made the representation had. However, if a good title is passed under this exception then that title is good against the whole world. (*Eastern Distributors Ltd v Goldring* [1957].) There is some doubt as to whether this exception is a true estoppel because generally an estoppel can operate only against the person who made the representation. For example, let us assume that A, the owner of goods, represents to B that C has the power to sell the goods. C does sell the goods to B. B will have become owner because A will be estopped from denying the truth of what he represented to B. Furthermore, if D claimed the goods, perhaps because he had later bought them from A, then B could raise this estoppel against D, even though D never made a representation.

SALE UNDER A VOIDABLE TITLE (SGA s.23)

A person who induces another to sell goods by making an actionable misrepresentation, or by means of duress or undue influence, will gain title to the goods. However, the title gained will be voidable. This means that the seller of the goods has the option to avoid the contract and render it void. (See *Contract Nutshell.*)

Section 23 SGA provides that if a person who has only a voidable title to goods resells the goods to an innocent third party **before** the original contract has been avoided then the third party will gain complete title to the goods. This is an exception to the *nemo dat* rule because the person who had the voidable title is giving what he did not have, he is giving complete title.

Example

Roger, a rogue, buys a car from Andrew. Andrew was induced to make the contract because of a fraudulent misrepresentation made by Roger. Roger has title to the car, but he has only a voidable title. Furthermore, this voidable title will soon become worthless when Andrew avoids the contract. Before Andrew avoids the contract Roger sells the car to Betty, an innocent third party acting in good faith. Betty has complete title to the car by virtue of s.23. Andrew is left with the right to sue Roger for damages.

If a person with a voidable title resells the goods to a third party **after** the title has been avoided then no title is passed on to the third party. This has nothing to do with s.23 SGA. It is just that once the title has been avoided there is no longer any title to pass on to the third party.

A person who has parted with goods under a contract which is voidable can avoid the contract by letting the other party know that the contract is no longer binding. The most effective way to do this is to tell the other party. If the other party is a rogue, who obtained the goods by means of a fraudulent misrepresentation, and the rogue can no longer be contacted, then *Car and Univeral Finance Co Ltd v Caldwell* [1964] held that performing an act which showed a definite intention not to be bound by the contract was sufficient to avoid it. In that case this was done by asking the police and the AA to keep a look out for the car. However, in *Car and Universal Finance* the Court of Appeal said that such a definite action might not be enough to avoid a contract induced by a negligent or innocent misrepresentation.

Section 23 will not be effective if the third party only agreed to buy the goods. It will be effective only if the third party has bought the goods. Only a third party who bought the goods in good faith, and without notice that the seller had only a voidable title, can benefit from s.23. However, this exception is different to all of the others in that here the original owner must prove that the third party did not act in good faith. With all the other exceptions the third party buyer must prove that he did act in good faith. If the third party buys the goods too cheaply then it may be possible for the original owner to show bad faith.

A third party who does not succeed under s.23 should always consider using s.25

This section, considered later in this chapter, allows a "buyer in possession" to pass a title which he did not have. We shall see that the requirements of s.25 are difficult to satisfy. However, a person who has acquired goods under a contract induced by misrepresentation, duress or undue influence will be a buyer in possession. This is not in itself enough to mean that he can pass a good title, but it does mean that this possibility should be considered.

SALE BY A SELLER IN POSSESSION AFTER A SALE (SGA s.24/FA s.8)

Section 24 SGA allows a seller in possession after a sale to pass a good title to a second buyer. Section 24 SGA reproduces s.8 Factors Act 1889 almost word for word. However, the wording in s.8 FA is slightly wider and so it is best to consider this section rather than s.24 SGA.

Section 8 FA 1889 applies where a seller of goods has already sold them to a buyer (Buyer 1). As the seller has sold the goods he no longer owns them. Buyer 1 owns them. If the seller keeps possession of the goods, or of the documents of title to the goods, and then sells the goods again to Buyer 2, Buyer 2 gets the title which had passed to Buyer 1, even though the seller no longer had ownership to pass.

Example

Farmer Steve sells his second-hand tractor to Bobby (Buyer 1). As these are specific goods in a deliverable state, Bobby immediately becomes owner of the tractor by virtue of s.18 Rule 1 SGA. Farmer Steve keeps possession of the tractor and sells it again to Billy (Buyer 2), who takes the tractor away. Billy becomes the owner of the tractor, even though Steve no longer had ownership to give at the time of the contract. Bobby is left with the right to sue Steve for non-delivery and to reclaim the price, on account of there having been a total failure of consideration.

There are several points to note. First, the seller must be in possession of the goods or of the documents of title at the time of the sale to the second buyer. However, s.1(2) FA 1889 provides that if the goods or documents are held by a person under the seller's control (such as an employee), or are held on the seller's behalf, then this is alright.

Second, although the seller needs to be in possession of the goods or documents, he does not need to be in possession in his capacity as seller. In *Pacific Motors Pty Ltd v Motor Credits (Hire Finance) Ltd* [1965] the sellers were in possession as agents, not as sellers, but nevertheless they could pass a good title.

Third, the seller must dispose of the goods to the second buyer under a "sale, pledge or other disposition". In *Worcester*

Works Finance Ltd v Cooden Engineering Co Ltd [1972] Lord Denning said that "disposition" was a very wide word. There would be a disposition whenever a new legal or equitable interest was created. However, he also said that merely giving the second buyer possession was not enough to amount to a disposition.

Fourth, the second buyer must take delivery of the goods or the documents of title, although constructive delivery will be good enough. (*Michael Gerson Leasing Ltd v Wilkinson* [2002].) Fifth, the second buyer must take in good faith and without notice.

If the requirements of s.8 FA 1889 are satisfied then the effect shall be "as if the person making the delivery or transfer were expressly authorised by the owner of the goods to make the same". This wording suggests that the second buyer would gain a good title against the whole world even if the original seller never had any title at all. However, the section has been interpreted to mean that the second buyer will gain the title which the original seller had, which had been passed to "the owner", the first buyer. If it were not interpreted in this way an absurd position would follow. For example, let us assume that a thief steals goods, and therefore has no ownership of them. The thief sells the goods to Buyer 1 who, of course, gains no ownership as the thief had no ownership to give. The thief retains possession of the goods and sells them to Buyer 2. A literal reading of s.24 would say that Buyer 2 owned the goods because the effect of satisfying s.8 would be as if the true owner of the goods had authorised the sale to Buyer 2. As this outcome is absurd, the courts have not interpreted s.8 to have this effect. No ownership will have passed to Buyer 2 and ownership will have remained with the true owner throughout. For the purposes of this section, Buyer 2 gets the title which Buyer 1, here regarded as "the owner" had.

BUYER IN POSSESSION AFTER A SALE (SGA s.25/FA s.9)

Both s.9 Factors Act 1889 and s.25 SGA allow a buyer in possession to pass title to goods even when he has not got title. As the wording of s.9 is slightly wider than that of s.25 SGA, it is this provision which is usually considered.

The idea behind s.9 is that a buyer, Buyer 1, has agreed to buy goods. Buyer 1 has obtained possession of the goods but has not yet acquired title. If Buyer 1 resells the goods to Buyer 2, then

Buyer 2 gets immediate ownership of the goods even though Buyer 1 did not have ownership to give.

Example

Benjamin has agreed to buy a car from Sally's garage. A retention of title clause (see Ch.4) provides that ownership of the car will not pass to Benjamin until he has paid the full price. Benjamin gets possession of the car and sells it to Brian. Brian will become owner of the car, even though Benjamin was never owner of it.

Although s.9 FA sounds simple enough, there are several technical requirements.

The first requirement is that the first buyer must have bought or agreed to buy the goods. This means that the provision will not work if the first buyer has taken the goods on hire-purchase. (*Helby v Mathews* [1895].) Nor will it work if the first buyer acquired the goods under a contract of sale or return or under a contract to provide services. The section will work if the first buyer has acquired goods under a credit sale. Whether or not it will work if the buyer has acquired the goods under a conditional sale depends upon whether or not the conditional sale was one requiring payment by instalments which was also within the Consumer Credit Act 1974. If the conditional sale is within the CCA 1974, and if at least some of the price is payable by instalments, then it is treated for the purposes of s.9 FA as hire-purchase and so s.9 cannot pass title to a second buyer. If the conditional sale was not within CCA 1974, or if none of the price was payable by instalments, then s.9 can pass title to a second buyer. A conditional sale is within the CCA 1974 if the buyer is not a company and the **credit** given is less than £25,000.

Example

Belinda agrees to buy a car from Sally's Garage. The contract is a conditional sale agreement to be paid by 24 monthly instalments, and property is not to pass until the final payment is made. After making only three payments Belinda sells the car to Bert, who does not know that Belinda does not yet own the car. If the conditional sale to Belinda was within the CCA 1974, because the credit given to Belinda was £25,000 or less, then s.9 FA cannot pass title to Bert. If the conditional sale to Belinda was not within the CCA 1974 then title will pass to Bert.

The second requirement is that the seller must have consented to the first buyer obtaining possession of the goods, or the documents of title, and the goods or documents of title must be delivered to the second buyer. Constructive delivery is good enough, as long as there is some voluntary act transferring possession.

Third, the delivery to the second buyer must be made under a sale, pledge or other disposition. The meaning of this will be the same as it was in relation to s.24/s.8. The wording of s.9 FA 1889 (but not of s.25 SGA) allow the second buyer to take under an agreement for sale. However, in *Re Highway Foods International Ltd* [1995] it was held that an agreement to sell to the second buyer would not pass title. This is because where there is a mere agreement to sell to the second buyer he would not acquire title anyway until the property was to pass to him.

Fourth, the second buyer can gain title under s.9 FA only if he takes the goods in good faith and without notice of the first buyer's defect of title.

Finally, *Newtons of Wembley Ltd v Williams* [1964] has added a requirement that when the first buyer sells or disposes of the goods, he must do so in the way in which a mercantile agent acting in the ordinary course of business of a mercantile agent would have done so. In the case the first buyer was rogue who had bought a car with a bad cheque. The second buyer could not take advantage of s.23 because the contract had been avoided by the time he bought the car. The second buyer did gain title under s.25 but only because the rogue happened to sell the car in the way in which a mercantile agent would have sold it. As most first buyers will not resell the goods in this way this case has severely limited the effect of s.25. In *Newtons of Wembley* the Court of Appeal took a very restrictive view of the wording of s.25/s.9. The last words of the sections say that, if all of the requirements of s.25/s.9 are satisfied, the effect shall be as if the first buyer was a mercantile agent in possession of the goods with the consent of the owner. Most people saw this as a long-winded way of saying that the effect shall be that the first buyer will pass ownership. However, in *Newtons of Wembley* the Court of Appeal interpreted the section literally to mean that the first buyer became a notional mercantile agent, in possession of the goods with the consent of the owner. Because a mercantile agent, in possession of goods with the consent of the owner, cannot pass title under s.2(1) FA unless he sells the goods in the ordinary course of business of a mercantile agent, a buyer in possession likewise cannot pass title unless he sells, or otherwise disposes of, the goods in the ordinary course of business of a mercantile agent. That is to say during business hours from business premises. The twelfth report of the Law Reform Committee criticised this decision as imposing an unnecessary restriction.

The title passed if s.9 is effective is only the title which the person who sold the goods to the first buyer had. If the person who sold to the first buyer had no title, perhaps because he had stolen the goods, then s.9 will not pass a good title to the second buyer. (*National General Insurance Association v Jones* [1990].)

SALE OF A MOTOR VEHICLE OBTAINED ON HIRE-PURCHASE (HPA 1964 s.27)

When considering the "buyer in possession" exception we saw that a person who has taken goods on hire-purchase has neither bought nor agreed to buy the goods. Ownership of the goods will not pass until the final instalment is paid. It follows that if a person taking goods on hire-purchase sells the goods before paying the final instalment then no title will pass to the buyer. However, the Hire Purchase Act 1964 makes an exception in the case of motor vehicles.

Example

John takes a fridge and a car on hire purchase. John immediately sells both to Mary, who takes them in good faith and without notice. Mary will not gain title to the fridge. John had no title to the fridge and cannot therefore pass title. Mary will gain title to the car under s.27 HPA 1964, as long as the requirements of that section are satisfied.

The requirements of s.27 HPA 1964 are as follows.

First, the section applies only to motor vehicles, defined as mechanically propelled vehicles adapted or intended for use on roads to which the public has access. So cars and motorbikes would be included, bicycles and caravans would not.

Second, the vehicle must have been subject to a hire-purchase agreement or a conditional sale agreement. When we considered buyer in possession above we saw that a conditional sale agreement is very similar to a hire-purchase agreement. The difference is that the buyer under a conditional sale has agreed to pay all of the instalments and to buy the goods, whereas a hire-purchaser has the option to pay all of the instalments and thereby buy the goods. Here there is no requirement that the conditional sale is subject to the Consumer Credit Act. Any conditional sale will do.

Third, the section can pass title only to a private purchaser. (Although this private purchaser, having become owner of the goods, can then pass title to anyone.) A person who acts as a part-time motor dealer cannot be regarded as a private purchaser, even if he buys the motor vehicle for his private use. (*Stevenson v Beverley Bentinck Ltd* [1976]. The good faith of the first private purchaser is the key to whether or not title passes. If the first private purchaser acted in good faith title will pass to him under the Act, and he can then pass title to others. If the first private purchaser did not act in good faith then no-one can gain title under the Act.

Fourth, the first private purchaser must buy the motor vehicle or take it on hire-purchase.

Example

Harry takes a car on hire-purchase from HP Ltd and immediately sells the car to Ace Garage Ltd. Ace Garage Ltd sell the car to Betta Garage Ltd, who sell it to Charles, a teacher. Charles sells the car to David, a doctor, who sells it to Easy Garage Ltd. Harry did not own the car and had no right to sell it because he had taken it on hire-purchase. Neither Ace Garage nor Betta Garage owned the car. The HPA 1964 would not pass ownership to them as they were not private purchasers. Charles was the first private purchaser and he would gain title to the car if he acted in good faith. Having gained title, Charles would pass title in the ordinary way to David who would pass it to Easy Garage Ltd. If Charles did not act in good faith then ownership of the car would never have moved from HP Ltd. David might have acted in good faith but he could not take advantage of the Act because he was not the first private purchaser.

The title passed under the Act is the title which the creditor who let the goods out on hire-purchase had. (In the example above, the title of HP Ltd.) If this creditor has no title then no title is passed under the Act.

MARKET OVERT (SGA s.22, ABOLISHED IN 1995)

Before 1995 if goods were sold in an established market between the hours of sunrise and sunset then title passed to the buyer, even if the goods were stolen. This exception has been abolished as regards contracts made after January 3, 1995.

Since the abolition of market overt none of the exceptions to the *nemo dat* rule can pass title in stolen goods. (You should of course realise that a rogue who has paid with a bad cheque has not stolen the goods and does obtain a voidable title to the goods.)

5. DUTIES OF THE SELLER AND THE BUYER

Overview

Section 27 SGA sets out the fundamental obligations of the parties to a contract of sale of goods. It tells us that the seller has one duty, to deliver the goods. It also tells us that the buyer has two duties, to accept the goods and to pay for them. The Act then deals with some fairly technical rules about delivery.

Unless otherwise agreed, delivery of the goods and the payment of the price are **concurrent conditions**. (Section 28.) This does not mean that delivery and payment must occur at the same. In the majority of commercial contracts they do not. What it means is that the seller must be ready and willing to give possession of the goods to the buyer in return for the price, and the buyer must be ready and willing to pay the price in exchange for possession of the goods. So if the seller said that he would not deliver the goods, the buyer would be entitled not to pay the price. In this case the buyer could sue the seller for damages for non-delivery but the seller could not sue for non-payment. The seller's unwillingness to deliver would allow the buyer to refuse to pay the price. However, any damages due to the buyer would take account of the fact that the price had not been paid. If the buyer said that he would not pay the price to a seller who was willing to deliver the goods, the seller could then refuse to deliver the goods. The seller **might** then be able to sue for the price, (see below). If the seller could not sue the buyer for the price, he could sue for damages for non-acceptance. Damages are considered in the following chapter.

DELIVERY

Meaning of delivery

Delivery is concerned with possession of the goods, not ownership of the goods. It means a voluntary transfer of possession from one person to another. (Section 61(1).) As regards the seller's duty to deliver the goods, delivery might either mean that the buyer must take possession of the goods or it might mean that the seller should send the goods to the buyer. This will depend upon the express or implied terms of the contract.

(Section 29(1).) Unless otherwise agreed, the expenses of putting the goods into a deliverable state must be borne by the seller. (Section 29(6).) If the seller does have the duty to send the goods to the buyer then they must be sent within a reasonable time, unless a time for sending them was fixed. (Section 29(3).)

Time of delivery

The time of delivery may be made either a condition or a warranty by the terms of the contract. (Section 10(2).) In commercial sales, case law has shown that the time of delivery, unlike the time of payment, is generally regarded as a condition. (*Bowes v Shand* [1877].) So if the seller tenders a late delivery the buyer can treat the contract as repudiated and refuse to accept the goods. Alternatively, the seller may treat the breach of condition as a breach of warranty. (Section 11(4).) A buyer who does this will lose the right to treat the contract as repudiated but will retain the right to sue for damages.

If the seller does not deliver on time, the buyer might waive his right to treat the contract as repudiated by indicating to the seller that he did not intend to treat the contract as repudiated. Having waived the right to treat the contract as repudiated, the buyer could reintroduce the right only by giving reasonable notice of an intention to do so. (*Charles Rickards v Oppenheim* [1950].)

If the time of delivery is not fixed in the contract then the seller must deliver within a reasonable time. (Section 29(3).) Even in such cases the seller will breach a condition by not delivering within a reasonable time. Likewise, if the buyer gives notice that the goods must be delivered within a certain reasonable time and they are not so delivered this will be a breach of condition. (*McDougall v Aeromarine of Emsworth Ltd* [1958].) What is a reasonable time is a question of fact. (Section 59.)

Place of delivery

The contract might fix a place of delivery. If it does not, then s.29(2) makes three rules about the place of delivery. First, if the goods are specific goods which both of the parties know, at the time of the contract, to be in a certain place then that place is the place of delivery. Second, as regards other goods, the place of delivery is the seller's place of business. Third, if the seller has not got a place of business the place of delivery is the seller's home address.

Example

Arthur buys a second-hand tractor which both he and the seller know is stuck in the mud on one of farmer Brian's fields. Arthur also buys a new car from Charles, a motor dealer. As regards both contracts, nothing was agreed about the place of delivery. The place of delivery of the tractor would be the place where the tractor is. The place of delivery of the car would be Charles' place of business. If Charles did not have a place of business the place of delivery of the car would be Charles' home address. Notice that in all three limbs of this example Arthur would have to go and collect the goods. The sellers would fulfil their duty to deliver merely by making the goods available at the place of delivery. Notice also that a contract term might have put the place of delivery elsewhere or have obliged the sellers to send the goods to Arthur.

If at the time of the contract the goods are being held by a third party then delivery occurs only when the third party acknowledges to the buyer that he is now holding the goods on the buyer's behalf. (Section 29(4).)

Tender of delivery

A seller has a duty to tender delivery at the time when the contract terms require delivery, and achieves this by expressing a readiness to deliver. Such a tender of delivery, like a demand for delivery, can be effective only if the delivery is to take place at a reasonable time of day. (Section 29(5).) What amounts to a reasonable time of day is a question of fact and will therefore differ from case to case.

Delivery of the wrong quantity

If the seller delivers a quantity of goods which is **less** than the quantity contracted for then the buyer has two choices: either to reject the goods; or to accept the goods which were delivered and pay for these at the contract rate. (Section 30(1).) As regards the goods which were not delivered the buyer can sue for damages for non-delivery.

If the seller delivers a quantity of goods which is **more** than the quantity contracted for the buyer is given two choices by s.30(2): either to reject the lot; or to accept the quantity which should have been delivered and reject the excess. Section 30(3) gives the buyer a third option; to accept all of the goods delivered and pay for the excess at the contract rate. If the buyer rejects any of the goods he can, as regards those goods, sue for damages for non-delivery. Nor does the buyer have to return rejected goods to the seller. It is enough that the buyer lets the seller know that the goods have been rejected. (Section 36.)

Where the buyer does not deal as a consumer then the rights of rejection given by ss.30(1) and (2) cannot be exercised if the excess or shortfall was so slight that it would be unreasonable for the buyer to reject. This section does not state that a buyer who deals as a consumer could reject in these circumstances but it does seem to imply this. The definition of dealing as a consumer was considered in Ch.2.

Example

Imran, a dealer in cereals, buys 100 tons of rice from James at £200 a ton and 100 tons of wheat from Giles at £20 a ton. James delivers 90 tons of rice and Giles delivers 105 tons of wheat. As regards the rice, Imran has two choices. Either reject all 90 tons delivered and have the right to sue for damages for non-delivery. Or accept the 90 tons delivered, pay £1,800 for it and have the right to sue for non-delivery of the shortfall. As regards the wheat, Imran has three choices. Either reject all 105 tons and have the right to sue for non delivery. Or take 100 tons and pay £2,000. Or take the whole 105 tons and pay £2,100.

All of the rules set out in s.30 can be varied by agreement between the parties, by trade usage or by a course of dealing between the parties.

Delivery by instalments

Unless otherwise agreed, a buyer of goods is not bound to accept delivery by instalments. (Section 31(1).) If a contract to deliver by instalments is regarded as one single, entire obligation then any breach of condition will entitle the buyer to call the contract off. If, as is more likely, a contract to deliver by instalments is regarded as giving rise to a series of obligations, the contract will be severable. Section 31(2) says that a contract is severable if the goods are to be delivered by stated instalments which are to be separately paid for. But even where the instalments are not to be separately paid for, a court would regard a contract as severable if this was what the parties had intended. As regards severable contracts, the question arises whether the buyer can reject future instalments because one or more instalments has been defective. If this breach is a repudiation of the whole contract then the buyer can reject all future instalments. If it is not a repudiation of the whole contract then the buyer can claim damages but cannot treat the whole contract as repudiated. Section 31(2) tells us that whether or not the breach is a repudiation of the whole contract will depend upon the terms of the contract and the circumstances of the case. *Maple Flock Co Ltd v Universal Furniture Products (Wembley) Ltd* [1934] held that the two most important circumstances are the ratio of the breach to the contract as a whole and the likelihood of the breach being repeated.

Delivery to a carrier

If the seller is authorised or required to send the goods to the buyer, delivery to a carrier (whether named by the buyer or not) for the purpose of transmission to the buyer is prima facie deemed to be delivery of the goods to the buyer. (Section 32(1).) In effect, s.32(1) makes the carrier the agent of the buyer. However, it is important to note that s.32(1) will not apply if the carrier is the agent or employee of the seller. Section 18 Rule 5(2) makes a similar rule, subject to contrary intention, as regards the unconditional appropriation of unascertained goods. (See Ch.3) It provides that delivery of the goods to a carrier for the purpose of transmission to the buyer is to be taken as an unconditional appropriation of the goods to the contract, unless the seller reserves the right of disposal. An unconditional appropriation of the goods to the contract would pass ownership of the goods to the buyer. It would also pass the risk unless the parties had agreed to separate the ownership and the risk. (See p.47.) However, neither s.18 Rule 5(2) nor s.32(1) can override s.16, which provides that property in the goods cannot pass to the buyer until the goods have been ascertained. Section 32(1) does not apply where the buyer deals as a consumer. In such cases delivery to a carrier is not delivery to the buyer. (Section 32(4).) Where the buyer deals as a consumer the goods remain at the seller's risk until they are delivered to the consumer. (Section 20(4).)

Section 32(2) provides that, unless otherwise authorised by the buyer, the seller must make such a contract with the carrier as is reasonable having regard to the nature of the goods and the circumstances of the case. If the seller does not do this, and this causes the goods to be lost or damaged in transit, the buyer can either refuse to treat delivery to the carrier as delivery to himself or can sue the seller for damages.

Example

(i) Buyer A, who deals as a consumer, orders a new television from X and agrees that X should send it to him. X gives a television to Carrier C, to take to buyer A, but the television is lost in transit. The television has not been delivered to A and remained at X's risk. A will not have to pay the price and may sue for damages for non-delivery if another television is not sent. X might be able to sue C in the tort of negligence.

(ii) Buyer B orders a ton of coal from X and authorises X to send it to him. The coal is lost while being delivered by an employee of X. Sections 18(5)(2) and 32(1) have no application as the employee is not a carrier. The coal remained at X's risk. B will not have to pay the price and may sue for damages for non-delivery if another ton of coal is not sent.

(iii) Buyer D orders a ton of wheat from X and authorises X to send it to him. X phones D and tells him that his ton of wheat has been bagged up and given to Carrier C for delivery to him. The wheat is damaged in transit. Section 16 is satisfied as the goods have been ascertained. Section 32(1) will regard the wheat as having been delivered to D and the property will have passed to D under s.18 Rule 5(2). Therefore D will have to pay the price of the wheat. D might be able to sue Carrier C for negligence.

(iv) As in (iii) above, but X arranges for delivery by a carrier in an open top vehicle and the wheat is damaged by rainfall. The contract of carriage made by X was not reasonable and this caused the damage. The buyer may therefore either claim that no delivery has been made (and sue for damages for non-delivery) or may accept the delivery and sue the seller for damages.

Where the seller agrees to deliver the goods at his own risk to a place other than where they were sold, then the buyer has to take any risk of deterioration which is necessarily incidental to the course of transit (unless otherwise agreed). (Section 33.) This rule is less significant that it might sound because it applies only to risks which are necessarily incidental to the course of transit. It would therefore apply only where there was something inherently dangerous about the method of transport or the nature of the goods, and would not absolve the seller from having to take reasonable care to ensure that the goods arrive safely. Nor would it help a seller who sold goods which perished before they arrived. When a seller sells perishable goods, to be delivered by a carrier, the goods must be in such a state that they will remain of satisfactory quality until they arrive. (*Mash & Murrell Ltd v Joseph Emmanuel Ltd* [1962].)

THE BUYER'S DUTIES

The duty to pay the price

As we have seen the buyer has a duty to pay the price, and must be ready and willing to do so in exchange for delivery of the goods.

How is the price fixed?

Generally, the price will have been agreed as a term of the contract. Section 8(1) recognises that the price might be expressly fixed, or that the contract may agree how the price is to be fixed, or that the price may be determined by a course of dealing between the parties. If the price is not fixed in one of these ways then s.8(2) provides that a reasonable price must be paid. What amounts to a reasonable price is a question of fact depending upon all the circumstances of the case. Although the SGA sets out these ways in which the price can be fixed it is important to remember that if the price cannot be fixed in one of these ways then the contract may be void for lack of certainty.

Example

X might buy a ton of coal from Y, agreeing a price of £100. (Here the price is fixed by the contract). Or X might buy a pile of coal at £100 a ton. (The price is fixed by a manner agreed in the contract.) Or X might buy five tons of coal from Y with no mention of the price. If X regularly buys coal from Y at £100 a ton, then this course of dealing will fix the price at £100 a ton. If

X has never previously bought coal from Y, then the court might be prepared to find what a reasonable price would have been and order that this price be paid. However, if a reasonable price could not be determined then the contract would be void for uncertainty.

Selling at a valuation

The parties to a contract of sale might agree that the price be fixed by a third party. Having made this agreement they will have to stick to it. However, s.9(1) provides that if the third party fails to make a valuation then the contract is void. If any of the goods have already been delivered, then the buyer must pay a reasonable price for them. Having made the agreement that a third party will fix the price, neither party must prevent the third party from doing this. A party who does prevent it will be liable to the other party in damages. (Section 9(2).)

The circumstances in which the seller may sue for the price are considered later in this chapter on p.79.

The duty to accept the goods

The buyer's duty to accept the goods means that he must not wrongfully reject them. A buyer who does wrongfully reject the goods has committed a repudiatory breach and can be sued for damages for non-acceptance under s.50. As wrongful non-acceptance is a repudiatory breach, it will absolve the seller from his duty to deliver. If the seller has already breached a condition, then the buyer will have the right to refuse to accept the goods. Such a refusal will therefore not mean that the buyer has wrongfully refused to accept.

The duty to take delivery

A refusal to accept is not necessarily the same thing as a refusal to take delivery. A refusal to accept is a repudiation of the contract. A wrongful refusal to take delivery might not be a repudiation of the contract. If it is not a repudiation it would make the buyer liable in damages under s.37, but would not allow the seller to terminate the contract. If by refusing to take delivery the buyer breaches a condition, or signifies a refusal to be bound by the contract, then this will amount to a repudiation of the contract. The seller could accept this repudiation, terminate the contract and claim damages for non-acceptance and non-delivery. Remedies are considered in the following chapter.

In relation to a breach of the statutory implied terms contained in ss.13–15, we considered the ways in which a buyer might be deemed by s.35 to have accepted the goods. We saw that a buyer who is deemed to have accepted the buyer can no longer reject the goods. The mere act of taking delivery does not amount to acceptance of the goods. It merely prevents the buyer from later claiming that the seller's tender of delivery was made in the wrong way or at the wrong time. If a buyer has a right to refuse to accept goods then this will also entitle him to refuse to take delivery of them.

Late payment

Late payment of the price is presumed to be a breach of warranty rather than a breach of condition. (Section 10(1).) It therefore entitles the seller to damages but not to repudiate the contract. There will be no breach, and so no right to damages, if the buyer pays within an agreed period of credit. The Late Payment of Commercial Debts (Interest) Act 1998 allow a supplier of goods or services to a business to charge a statutory rate of interest if the price is paid late.

RIGHTS OF THE UNPAID SELLER

AN ACTION FOR THE PRICE

Section 49(1) provides that the seller may sue the buyer for the price if the property in the goods has passed to the buyer and the buyer wrongfully neglects or refuses to pay for the goods according to the terms of the contract. The circumstances in which property has passed to the buyer were considered in Ch.4.

Section 49(2) allows the seller to sue for the price, even if the property in the goods has not passed to the buyer, as long as the contract set a definite date for payment. If the property in the goods has not passed to the buyer, and the contract sets no definite date for payment, then the seller cannot sue for the price. (*Colley v Overseas Exporters Ltd* [1921].) However, the seller will be able to sue for damages if the buyer wrongfully refuses to take delivery or wrongfully refuses to accept the goods. (Both of these matters were considered earlier in this chapter.)

UNPAID SELLER'S RIGHTS AGAINST THE GOODS

An unpaid seller is given three rights against the goods. As these rights are taken against the goods, rather than against the buyer, they are regarded as **real rights** not personal rights.

Definition of an unpaid seller

Section 38(1) defines a seller as unpaid when: (a) the whole of the purchase price has not been paid or tendered; or (b) a negotiable instrument (such as a cheque) which has been given as payment has been dishonoured. A seller can be an unpaid seller where he has given the buyer credit (although not all of the real remedies will then be available). Even a seller who has been paid some of the price can be an unpaid seller.

The unpaid seller's lien (s.41)

The unpaid seller's lien entitles an unpaid seller to keep possession of the goods until the price has been paid or tendered. There are, however, two restrictions. First the seller must actually have possession of the goods, although he may have possession as the buyer's agent or bailee. Second, the right will not arise where the buyer has been given credit and the period of credit has not expired. The right arises automatically if the buyer becomes insolvent. Technically, a lien can arise only if the property had passed to the buyer. However, s.39(2) provides that where the property has not passed to the buyer the seller has a similar right to withhold delivery.

Example

Bertha buys a consignment of wheat from Sally. Bertha is not given credit. Sally can refuse to let Bertha have possession of the wheat until the whole price has been paid or tendered.

The unpaid seller's lien can be lost by delivering the goods to a carrier or other bailee for transmission to the buyer, unless the seller reserves a right of disposal of the goods. (A reservation of title clause would reserve the right of disposal, see p.49, as would the seller taking out a bill of lading in his own name, see p.105.) It can be lost if the buyer or his agent lawfully gains possession of the goods, even if the unpaid seller regains possession. It is also lost if the seller waives the lien. (Section

43.) Obviously, it is lost if the buyer pays the full price of the goods.

A seller who has made part delivery of goods can exercise a lien over the remainder, unless the circumstances show that the part delivery waived this right to exercise a lien over the remainder. (Section 42.)

The exercise of a line does not of itself rescind the contract. So if buyer, or his liquidator or trustee in bankruptcy, later pays the price the seller must deliver the goods.

Stoppage in transit (s.44)

Section 44 gives an unpaid seller a right of stoppage in transit, which arises only if the buyer has become insolvent. It allows an unpaid seller who has parted with the goods to a carrier, for the purpose of taking them to the buyer, to stop the goods in transit and retake possession of them. Stoppage in transit is available whether or not the property in the goods has passed to the buyer. The right is lost once the goods are delivered to the buyer or his agent. (Section 45(2).) Stoppage in transit can be exercised either by taking actual possession of the goods or by giving notice to the carrier. (Section 46.) It does not terminate the contract (s.48(1)) and so the seller's trustee in bankruptcy or liquidator can still enforce the contract. Once stoppage in transit is exercised the carrier must re-deliver the goods to the seller, or according to the seller's instructions, and the seller must pay the expense of this. (Section 46(4).) A carrier who does not exercise stoppage in transit when ordered to do so will be liable in the tort of conversion to the unpaid seller.

Example

Stephen has sold a consignment of goods to Brian and given the goods to a carrier for delivery to Brian. Stephen, who has not yet been paid for the goods, then learns that Brian has become insolvent. Stephen contacts the carrier on a mobile phone and orders that the goods are brought back to him. As long as the goods have not yet been delivered to Brian the carrier must bring the goods back to Stephen and Stephen must pay the expense of this.

Sub-sale by the buyer

Section 47(1) provides that an unpaid seller's rights of lien and stoppage in transit are not affected by the buyer having sold the goods on to a sub-buyer, unless the seller had assented to this sub-sale.

Example

Sam, an unpaid seller, has sold goods to Brian. Brian has sold the goods on to Charlie, but Sam has not assented to this. Sam can exercise a lien over the goods, or stoppage in transit, despite the sub-sale to Charlie.

If a buyer gets the documents of title to the goods, and transfers these to a third party sub-buyer who is acting in good faith, then the unpaid seller's rights of stoppage in transit and lien are defeated. (Section 47(2).) As we have seen, both the right of lien and stoppage in trasnsit will be defeated if the buyer gets actual possession of the goods.

Unpaid seller's right of resale (s.48)

Section 48(1) provides that the mere fact of a seller exercising a right of lien, or stoppage in transit, does not rescind the contract of sale. However, if the unpaid seller, having exercised a right of lien or stoppage in transit, resells the goods then the new buyer gains a good title. (Section 48(2)). (A seller who resells goods which are still in his possession may also pass title to the second buyer as a seller in possession, a matter considered in Ch.4 on p.64.) So in these circumstances the unpaid seller has **the power** to pass a good title to a third party buyer. This is not the same as having **the right** to resell the goods. A seller with the power to pass good title, but no right to resell, would be liable in damages to the original buyer. A seller who has the right to resell will not be liable in damages to the original buyer and, indeed, may be able to sue the original buyer for damages.

The unpaid seller has **the right** to resell the goods and claim damages from the original buyer in four circumstances. First, where the goods are perishable and the buyer does not tender or pay the price within a reasonable time (s.48(3)). Second, where the unpaid seller givers the buyer notice of an intention to re-sell and the buyer does not tender or pay the price within a reasonable time (s.48(3)). Third, where the unpaid seller expressly reserves a right of resale. Fourth, where the buyer has repudiated the contract and the seller accepts this repudiation.

6. REMEDIES

REMEDIES OF THE SELLER AGAINST THE BUYER

The seller is given three personal remedies by the SGA; to sue for the price; to sue for damages for the buyer not taking delivery; or to sue for non-acceptance. As these remedies are taken against the buyer, rather than against the goods themselves, they are known as personal rather than real remedies. An unpaid seller also has rights in relation to the goods. These rights, sometimes known as real remedies, were considered in the previous chapter.

An action for the price

Section 49(1) provides that the seller can sue for the price if the property in the goods has passed to the buyer and the buyer wrongfully neglects or refuses to pay according to the terms of the contract. So if the property has not yet passed to the buyer then the seller cannot ordinarily sue for the price. *Colley v Overseas Exporters Ltd* [1921] provides an example. A buyer of a quantity of leather wrongfully failed to nominate the ship on which the goods were to be loaded. The leather was therefore left lying in the docks. The seller's claim for the price failed because the property had not yet passed to the buyer. However, s.49(2) makes one exception, allowing the seller to sue for the price even where the property has not yet passed, if the price was payable on a "day certain irrespective of delivery". This provision is necessary because if the contract provided that the buyer should pay the price before delivery, the seller would otherwise have no remedy if the seller failed to pay. (Assuming that the seller could not sue for the price because the property had not yet passed.) The seller could not sue for damages because the buyer would not yet have been obliged to accept or take delivery of the goods. In *Colley v Overseas Exporters Ltd* the seller could sue for damages for non-acceptance because the buyer had breached his duty to accept the goods.

Damages for non-acceptance

We have seen in the previous chapter that it is the duty of the buyer to accept the goods and pay for them. If the buyer breaches this duty, the seller can bring an action for damages for non-acceptance. This right could be exercised instead of suing for the price. It arises whether or not the property in the goods has passed to the buyer.

Section 50(1) merely states that the seller can sue for damages for non-acceptance if the buyer wrongfully neglects to accept and pay for the goods. The right arises only if the buyer's refusal to accept and pay is wrongful. The buyer might be entitled to refuse to accept the goods if, for example, they were faulty or delivered late or in the wrong place. In such as case the seller would have no right to damages (and the buyer would have such a right).

Having decided that the seller has a right to damages for non-acceptance we then have to ask whether there was an available market for the goods in question. If there was not, the measure of damages is the estimated loss directly and naturally resulting in the ordinary course of events from the buyer's breach of contract. (Section 50(2).) That is to say the loss is calculated according to the first Rule in *Hadley v Baxendale* [1854]. Loss of profit would be the most common type of claim which a business seller would make under s.50(2). The seller cannot claim for losses which could have been mitigated by taking reasonable steps.

If there was an available market for the goods in question then s.50(3) gives us a market rule. This says that prima facie the measure of damages is the amount by which the contract price is greater than the market or current price at the time when the goods ought to have been accepted. If no time was fixed for acceptance then it is the amount by which the contract price is greater than the market price at the time of refusal to accept.

The following diagram shows how s.50 should be approached.

There is an available market for goods if another buyer for the goods could reasonably be found and if the price of the goods would be set by the laws of supply and demand. But because the market rule is only a prima facie rule it is not always applied. It would not be applied if there was a much greater supply of the goods in question. In such a case the seller has still lost a sale, even if the goods had a market price and even if they could have been sold to another buyer. The market rule is a rule of mitigation and assumes that the seller will mitigate any loss by selling in the market. However, it will apply even if the seller fails to do this.

Figure 6.1

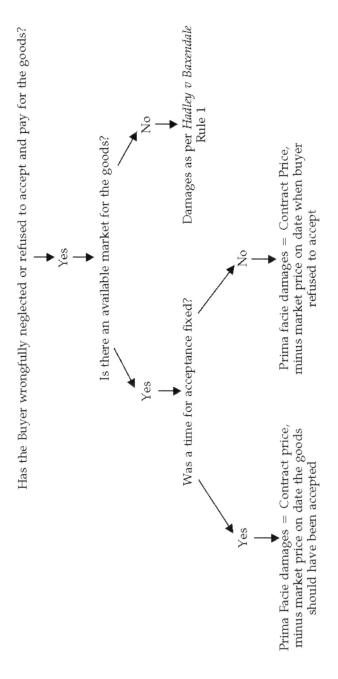

Has the Buyer wrongfully neglected or refused to accept and pay for the goods?

Yes

Is there an available market for the goods?

No → Damages as per *Hadley v Baxendale* Rule 1

Yes

Was a time for acceptance fixed?

No → Prima facie damages = Contract Price, minus market price on date when buyer refused to accept

Yes → Prima Facie damages = Contract price, minus market price on date the goods should have been accepted

Example

Susan sold 100 tons of wheat to Belinda, delivery to be made on April 10. The contract price was £10,000. On April 10, Belinda wrongfully refused to accept and pay for the wheat. If on April 10 the market price of wheat such as this was £10,000, or above £10,000, Belinda will be entitled to only nominal damages for non-acceptance. If on April 10 the market price was £8,000 then prima facie Belinda's damages for non-acceptance would be £2,000. The fact that Belinda did not go into the market to resell her wheat would make no difference to the amount of damages, no matter how the market price subsequently changed.

In addition to damages under the market rule, the seller might be able to claim special damages for other costs which were reasonably incurred. Section 54 allows such special damages to be claimed under *Hadley v Baxendale* Rule 2 if they were in the contemplation of the parties as likely to arise at the time of the contract.

Damages for refusal to take delivery

Section 37 allows a seller who is ready and willing to deliver the goods to claim damages if the buyer does not take delivery within a reasonable time. The section allows the seller to claim for losses which were caused by the delay in taking delivery, such as the cost of continuing to store the goods or continuing to insure them. Damages for these matters could be included in a claim under s.50 and so s.37 is generally of relevance only where the seller sues for the price.

Right to treat the contract as terminated

If the buyer repudiates the contract then the seller can accept the repudiation and treat the contract as terminated. This would not prevent the seller from suing for the price or for damages. It would merely mean that the seller had no further obligation to perform the contract.

REMEDIES OF THE BUYER

The buyer has two possible actions for damages, either for non-delivery or for breach of warranty. In addition, the buyer may be able to treat the contract as terminated and reject the goods.

Damages for non-delivery

Section 51(1) provides that where the seller wrongfully neglects or refuses to deliver the goods to the buyer the buyer may sue for damages for non-delivery. The buyer will also be able to sue for damages for non-delivery if goods which were delivered are rightfully rejected by the buyer. (In effect, the goods have been undelivered.)

Example

John buys a new car from Ian Garage Ltd. A car is delivered but it does not correspond with the description by which it was sold. John rejects the car and terminates the contract under s.13 SGA. John can bring an action for damages for non-delivery.

Having decided that a buyer can sue for damages for non-delivery, the next question is to ask whether there was an available market for the goods. If there was no available market, then s.51(2) provides that the damages are the estimated loss directly and naturally resulting, in the ordinary course of events from the seller's breach of contract. That is to say that damages will be assessed under the common law, as per *Hadley v Baxendale* Rule 1. The buyer has a duty to take reasonable steps to mitigate the los and will not be able to claim for losses which could have been mitigated by taking reasonable steps. Under s.51(2) buyers commonly claim for loss of profit, loss of goodwill or for damages they themselves have had to pay to their sub-buyers. However, such losses can be claimed only if the buyers have actually suffered the losses in question. If there was an available market then s.51(3) sets out a prima facie market rule. The damages will be the amount by which the market price exceeds the contract price at the time when the goods should have been delivered or, if no time was fixed for delivery, at the time of the refusal to deliver. (See Figure 6.2.) The market rule is a rule of mitigation, which assumes that the buyer will enter the market, on the date when delivery should have been made, and buy an alternative supply of goods. The fact that the buyer does not do this will not alter the amount of damages.

The following diagram shows how s.51 should be approached.

Figure 6.2

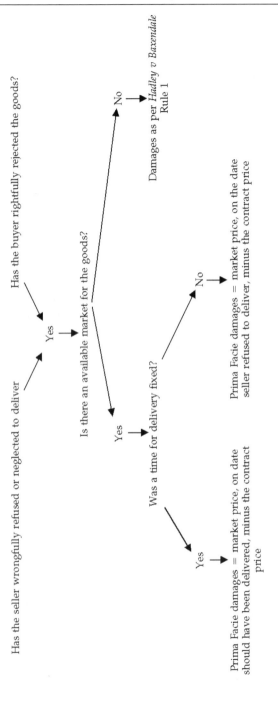

Example

Kenny has ordered 50 tons of wheat from MacDuncan at £50 a ton. Delivery was due on September 1 but MacDuncan wrongfully refused to deliver. There was an available market for wheat such as this on September 1. If the market price of wheat was £50 a ton or lower on September 1 then prima facie Kenny is entitled to only nominal damages for non-delivery. If the market price was £60 a ton then prima facie Kenny will be entitled to damages of £500 for non-delivery. Whether or not Kenny went into the market to buy an alternative supply of wheat would make no difference to his damages for non-acceptance.

In addition to damages under the market rule, the buyer might be able to claim special damages for other costs which were reasonably incurred. Section 54 allows such special damages to be claimed under *Hadley v Baxendale* Rule 2 if they were in the contemplation of the parties as likely to arise at the time of the contract.

Damages for breach of warranty

If the seller commits a breach of warranty then s.53(1) allows the buyer to sue for damages for breach of warranty or to deduct the amount of such damages from the price. It also gives the buyer these two choices if the buyer elects to treat a breach of condition as a breach of warranty. Section 11(4) compels a buyer who has accepted the goods to treat a breach of condition as a breach of warranty. This section is considered later in this chapter, along with the ways in which a buyer can be deemed to have accepted. Generally though, the buyer does not have to treat a breach of condition as a breach of warranty. Instead, the buyer may reject the goods for breach of condition and then sue for damages for non-delivery, as explained above.

Having decided that a buyer is entitled to damages for breach of warranty, s.53 then makes a distinction between breaches of warranty of quality and other breaches of warranty. If the breach relates to the quality of the goods then s.53(3) provides that the damages are the difference between the value the goods actually had when delivered and the value they would have had if there had been no breach of warranty. Generally, the value the goods would have had if there had been no breach of warranty will be the contract price.

Example

Parvinder buys a new car from X Garage Ltd for £10,000. The car is not of satisfactory quality and this makes it worth only £8,500. As s.14(2) has been breached, a condition has been breached and Parvinder could reject the goods, terminate the contract and sue for damages for non-delivery. However, Parvinder decides to treat the breach of condition as a breach of warranty and sue for damages for breach of warranty. The breach of warranty relates to the quality of the goods. So Parvinder's damages will prima facie be the value which the car would have had if there had been no breach of warranty (presumably, £10,000) less the amount which the car was actually worth (£8,500.) So prima facie the damages would be £1,500.

If the breach of warranty does not relate to the quality of the goods then s.53(2) tells us that the measure of damages is the estimated loss directly and naturally resulting, in the ordinary course of events, from the breach of warranty. That is to say, the damages are to be assessed under *Hadley v Baxendale* Rule 1.

The following diagram shows how s.53 should be approached.

The SGA 1979 makes no specific rule about damages for **late delivery**. If by delivering late the seller breaches a condition, which will generally be the case, the buyer may terminate the contract and sue for damages for non-delivery. But if the late delivery is only a breach of warranty, or if the buyer chooses to accept a late delivery, then damages for delayed delivery are assessed under common law principles, using the two Rules in *Hadley v Baxendale*. If the goods were for resale, the measure of damages is likely to be the amount by which the market price of the goods on the date they were actually delivered was lower than the price on the date on which they should have been delivered. If the goods were for use by the buyer then the buyer might be able to claim damages for the hire of alternative goods, as he would be expected to mitigate his loss by hiring alternative goods. If hiring alternative goods was not possible, the damages would generally be for profit lost on account of not having the goods during the period of delay.

Section 52 allows a court to order **specific performance** where the seller is in breach of a an obligation to deliver specific or ascertained goods. For the nature of specific performance, and the circumstances in which it will not be ordered, see *Nutshell on Contract*.

Figure 6.3

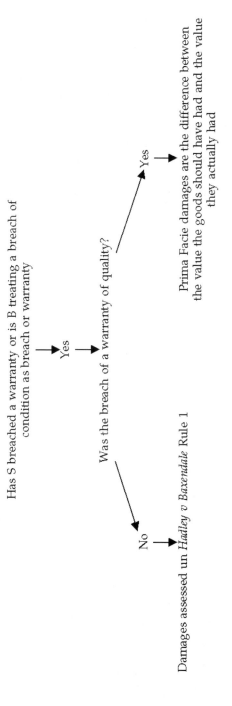

Has S breached a warranty or is B treating a breach of condition as breach or warranty

Yes

Was the breach of a warranty of quality?

Yes

Prima Facie damages are the difference between the value the goods should have had and the value they actually had

No

Damages assessed un *Hadley v Baxendale* Rule 1

THE BUYER'S RIGHT TO REJECT THE GOODS

A buyer can reject the goods in several circumstances. First, if the seller has breached a condition. Second, if the seller has delivered the wrong quantity of goods. Third, if the seller has repudiated the contract and the buyer accepts this repudiation. Fourth, if a term of the contract gives a right to reject. Fifth, if the seller has breached an innominate term and this has deprived the buyer of substantially the whole benefit of the contract. A mere breach of warranty will not entitle the buyer to reject the goods. The SGA 1979 labels some terms as condition and others as warranties. For a more general explanation of the differences between conditions, warranties and innominate terms see *Nutshell on Contract*.

Buyers who do not deal as consumers

Where the breach is of a statutory implied term, or consists of delivery of the wrong quantity, special rules apply in the case of buyers who do not deal as consumers. We saw in Ch.2 that if the breach of condition is a breach of ss.13, 14 or 15 then a buyer who does not deal as a consumer will not be entitled to reject of the breach was so slight that it would be unreasonable to reject. Instead, s.15A requires the buyer to treat the breach of condition as a breach of warranty. Thus damages will be available, but the right to reject will not. Similarly, in Ch.5 we saw that if the wrong quantity is delivered, a buyer who does not deal as a consumer cannot reject if the breach is so slight as to make rejection unreasonable. Again, the buyer must treat the breach of condition as a breach of warranty.

No need to return the goods

Section 36 provides that a buyer who rejects goods does not have to return them to the seller but only has to let the seller know that they have been rejected.

As we have seen, a buyer who rightfully rejects goods can sue for damages for non-delivery. A buyer who wrongfully rejects goods will repudiate the contract. The seller can then terminate the contract and sue for damages for non-acceptance.

Losing the right to reject

A buyer may waive a breach of condition or elect to treat it as a breach of warranty. Having done so, the buyer will not be able to treat the contract as repudiated but will still be able to claim damages. (Section 11(2).)

Acceptance by the buyer

Section 11(4) provides that where the contract of sale is not severable, a buyer who has accepted the goods or part of them will have to treat a breach of condition as a breach of warranty. So the right to damages will remain but the right to reject the goods and treat the contract as terminated will not.

Example

William buys a car from a garage. The car is not of satisfactory quality. William accepts the car. William will still be able to sue for damages under s.53 but will not be able to reject the car and treat the contract as terminated.

How is acceptance made?

Section 35 sets out three ways in which a buyer will be deemed to have accepted the goods. The first of these is contained in s.35(1)(a) which provides that a buyer will be deemed to accept if he **intimates to the seller that he has accepted**. The second way is contained in s.35(1)(b) which provides that the buyer is deemed to have accepted when the goods have been delivered to him and he **does any act which is inconsistent with the ownership of the seller**. At first, this seems rather odd as the buyer will be the owner of the goods if the property has passed to him. So he could well be expected to do many acts which are inconsistent with the seller owning the goods. What the section means is that the buyer must not do any act which would be inconsistent with the seller's rights to get the goods back if the buyer decides to reject. (*Kwei Tek Chao v British Traders and Shippers Ltd* [1954].) For example, if I bought a car which was delivered to me, ownership of the car would be with me not the seller. If the car was not of satisfactory quality, I could reject it under s.14. But if I re-sprayed the car I would be deemed to have accepted it and could no longer reject it. This would be because the act of re-spraying it would be inconsistent with the seller's right to get the goods back, in much the same condition as when sold, if I should reject the car. I would, of course, still be able to claim damages under s.53.

As regards both of the methods of acceptance set out in s.35(1), a buyer to whom goods have been delivered cannot be deemed to have accepted them until he has had a reasonable opportunity of examining them to see that they are in conformity with the contract. (Section 35(2).) A buyer who deals as a consumer cannot lose this right, (s.35(3).)

The third way in which the buyer can be deemed to have accepted is set out in s.35(4). It provides that the buyer is deemed to have accepted the goods **when after the lapse of a reasonable time he retains the goods without intimating to the seller that he has rejected them**. For example, if I buy a fridge which is not of satisfactory quality I will not be able to reject it two years later, as I will be deemed to have accepted it. (The right to sue for damages under s.53 would remain.) What amounts to a reasonable time is a question of fact. (Section 59.) It is up to a court to decide whether the buyer has retained the goods for more than a reasonable time. However, s.35(5) states that one factor to be considered is whether the buyer has had a reasonable opportunity to examine the goods to see that they are in conformity with the contract.

If the buyer sells the goods onto a sub-buyer, this is obviously inconsistent with the ownership of the original seller. However, s.35(6) that a buyer will not be deemed to have accepted **merely** because he does this or **merely** because he asks the seller to repair the goods. In *Clegg v Olle Andersson* [2003] it was held that where a buyer was awaiting information which the seller had agreed to supply, which would enable the buyer to make a properly informed choice between acceptance, rejection or cure, the buyer could not have lost his right to reject. In *Jones v Gallagher* [2004] it was suggested that this is not an absolute rule. If it were, it would conflict with the overall principle of the SGA, that assessment of the loss of the right to reject is a matter of fact to be considered in the light of all of the circumstances.

Rejecting some of the goods

If the goods form a **commercial unit** then a buyer who accepts any goods in the unit is deemed to have accepted all of the goods in the unit. A commercial unit means a unit division of which would materially impair the value of the goods or the character of the unit. (Section 35(7).)

Example

George buys a set of encyclopaedias, one volume to be delivered a month for 26 months. The first six volumes are of satisfactory quality but the seventh volume is not. George cannot reject any of the volumes because the full set makes a commercial unit and he has accepted some of the goods in the unit. George could, of course, claim damages.

If goods which do not form a commercial unit are delivered under a contract which is not severable then s.35A sets out the buyer's right to reject part of the goods. If all of the goods are affected by the breach then the buyer can either reject all of the goods or reject some of the goods. If only some of the goods are affected by the breach the buyer can either: reject all of the goods; or reject all of the goods which did not conform to the contract; or reject some of the goods which did not conform to the contract. If the buyer accepts any of the goods, he cannot reject goods which did conform to the contract.

Example

Benjamin buys 100 bags of wheat. The wheat is delivered but 10 bags are not of satisfactory quality. Benjamin can reject all 100 bags, or reject the 10 non-conforming bags, or reject some of the 10 non-conforming bags. If he accepts any of the bags he cannot reject any of the 90 bags which did conform to the contract. As regards bags which were rejected, Benjamin can sue for damages for non-delivery under s.51. As regards non-conforming bags which were accepted, he can sue for damages for breach of warranty under s.53.

Terminating the contract

Generally, a buyer who rejects the goods will also terminate the contract. There is some dispute as to whether or not the buyer can rightfully reject unascertained goods without terminating the contract. It seems likely that this is possible, so that the seller can subsequently deliver alternative goods as long as these match the contract description and are delivered within the contract period.

Rejection in contracts other than sales of goods

The rules on rejection outlined above do not apply unless the contract can be classified as a sale of goods. The definition of a contract of sale of goods was considered in Ch.1. In contracts other than sales of goods, (such as contracts of hire, hire-purchase, to transfer property in goods or to provide a service,) a breach of condition or a repudiation by the supplier will enable the customer to treat the contract as terminated. However, this right will be lost once the contract has been **affirmed**. There is no statutory definition of what is meant by affirmation. Cases indicate that affirmation takes place when the customer, knowing of the breach, indicates that he will not be treating the contract as repudiated. Having affirmed the contract, the customer can no longer treat it as terminated but can claim damages for the breach. If the customer does rightfully treat the contract as repudiated then all of the price can be claimed back only if there was a total failure of consideration. If there was a partial failure of consideration then only some of the amount paid can be reclaimed. In *Jones v Callagher* [2004] the Court of Appeal applied the SGA rules on acceptance to a contract which it had classified as a contract to transfer property in goods, rather than as a contract of sale of goods. This seems to have been an oversight rather than an indication of future policy.

ADDITIONAL RIGHTS OF BUYERS IN CONSUMER CASES

Sections 48A–F give buyers who deal as consumers **additional rights** if the goods did not conform to the contract at the time of delivery. The circumstances in which a buyer deals as a consumer were examined in Ch.2 on p.28. Before considering the effect of s.48A–F you should always check that the buyer dealt as a consumer.

Section 48F provides that goods do not conform to the contract if either an express term was breached or if a term implied by ss.13, 14 or 15 was breached. If the goods do not conform to the contract within six months of the date of delivery then there is a presumption that the goods did not conform at the date of delivery. (Section 48A(3).) This presumption would not apply if the seller could prove that the goods did conform at the date of delivery, nor if the presumption would be incompatible with the nature of the goods or the nature of the lack of conformity. (Section 48A(4).)

Example

Sarah, while dealing as a consumer, makes two contracts. First, she buys a new television. Second, she buys a dozen eggs. Three months later the television cannot be turned on and the eggs have gone bad. Sarah will gain the additional rights as regards the television because it will be presumed that the goods did not conform at the time of the contract. Because of the nature of the goods, and the nature of the lack of conformity, it will not be presumed that the eggs failed to conform at the time of delivery. Sarah will gain the additional rights only if she can prove that the eggs did not in fact conform at the time of delivery. If Sarah had not dealt as a consumer then she would not have gained the additional rights in respect of either the television or the eggs.

The hierarchy of rights

The rights gained under ss.48A–F are in two tiers. A buyer who qualifies, on account of having dealt as a consumer while buying goods which do not conform to the contract, has a right to choose either of the two remedies in the first tier. **These first tier remedies are the rights to repair** or **replacement of the goods**. (Section 48B(1).) Once the buyer has made the choice of repair or replacement then s.48B(2)(a) requires the seller to perform the remedy within a reasonable time and without causing significant inconvenience to the buyer. The cost of doing this must be borne by the seller. (Section 48B(2)(b).) What is a reasonable time is a question of fact. (Section 59.) However, when deciding what is a reasonable time in this context, or what is significant inconvenience, s.48B(5) says that reference must be made (a) to the nature of the goods and (b) to the purpose for which they were acquired. If the buyer does request either repair or replacement then he must not change his mind and go for the other remedy, or reject the goods and terminate the contract, until the seller has been given a reasonable time to perform the remedy requested. (Section 48D.)

Example

Jane, dealing as a consumer, buys a new car which did not conform to the contract as it was not of satisfactory quality. Jane can either ask the seller to repair or replace the car. Jane elects to go for repair. Until she has given the seller a reasonable time to effect the repair, Jane can neither reject the car for breach of the condition set out in s.14(2) nor change her mind and ask for replacement of the car.

Section 48B(3) provides that the buyer must not require repair or replacement if the remedy requested is impossible or disproportionate in comparison to any of the four remedies given by ss.48A–F. That is to say, disproportionate in relation to the other first tier remedy or in relation to the two second tier remedies. Section 48B(4) tells us that a remedy is disproportionate if it imposes costs on the seller which are unreasonable compared with the costs which would be imposed by another of the remedies. In assessing this, account should be taken of: (a) the value which the goods would have if they did conform to the contract of sale; (b) the significance of the lack of conformity; and (c) whether the other remedy could be effected without significant inconvenience to the buyer. So, to extend the example above, Jane would not be able to request repair of the car if the repair would be extremely costly in comparison to replacement of the car.

Section 48C(1) provides that the **second tier remedies are reducing the purchase price by an appropriate amount** or **rescission of the contract.** These remedies are not available as of right. They are available only if: the buyer cannot require repair or replacement because this is impossible or disproportionate to another remedy (s.48C(2)(a)); or the buyer has requested repair or replacement but the seller has breached his s.48B(2)(a) requirement to provide this within a reasonable time and without significant inconvenience to the buyer. Rescission in this context does not have its usual meaning because s.48C(3) tells us that if the buyer rescinds he may not get the full purchase price back. His reimbursement may be reduced to take account of any use of the goods he has had since the goods were delivered to him. If the remedy granted is reduction of the purchase price, the Act gives no indication as to how the amount of the reduction should be calculated.

Example

Mike, dealing as a consumer, buys a second hand car. Four months later Mike finds that the car is not of satisfactory quality. Mike asks the seller to repair the car. The seller cannot do this as he does not have the expertise and cannot arrange for anyone else to repair it. A replacement is not available as the car was specific goods. Mike can choose to rescind the car or to have the price reduced. If he chooses to rescind, he may not get all of the purchase price back. The court might deduct an amount to reflect the use of the car which he had had.

Section 48E gives the court wide power to substitute any of the four remedies for any another, or to order a remedy on such conditions as it sees fit.

Additional rights in other contracts

The SGSA 1982 gives identical additional rights to buyers in contracts for the transfer of property in goods. The rights do not apply to contracts of hire.

7. INTERNATIONAL SALES

In this chapter we consider two types of international sales contracts in some detail; free on board (FOB) contracts and cost, insurance and freight (CIF) contracts. We consider other types of contracts in outline. Before considering these different types of contracts we examine the legal effect of a document which is central to international sales, the bill of lading.

Throughout this chapter reference is made to the SGA 1979. This is because whenever goods are imported or exported, and English law governs the contract, then the provisions of the SGA 1979 will apply.

BILL OF LADING

A bill of lading is a document issued to a shipper of goods (usually the seller but possibly the buyer) by a shipowner. It states that goods of a certain description have been loaded on board the ship. The bill will also contain the terms and conditions of the contract of carriage. Often a **mate's receipt**, rather than a bill of lading, is given to the shipper when the goods are loaded on board. The details on the mate's receipt are then inserted into a bill of lading, which is given to the shipper before the ship leaves the port of loading.

There are three ways in which a bill of lading might have legal significance. First, it is evidence of the terms of the contract of carriage. Second, it acts as a receipt for the goods which have been loaded on board. Third, it is a document of title.

Bill of lading as evidence of the contract of carriage

A bill of lading reproduces the terms of the contract of carriage. However, the bill of lading is not itself the contract of carriage. The contract of carriage will have been made before the bill of lading is issued, when the ship was booked to carry the goods. As the bill of lading is not issued until, at the earliest, the time when the goods are loaded on board it follows that the bill of lading cannot itself be the contract of carriage.

As between the shipper and the shipowner, the bill of lading is very strong evidence as to the terms and conditions of the contract of carriage. It is therefore possible to introduce stronger evidence which shows that the contract of carriage was made on terms different to those contained in the bill of lading. (*The Ardennes v SS Ardennes* [1950].) However, as soon as the bill of lading is transferred to a third party it becomes conclusive evidence of the contract of carriage, so that it will not be possible to argue that the bill did not accurately state the terms agreed in the contract of carriage. This rule protects third parties to whom the bill is transferred (usually the buyer of the goods). The third party takes the contract of carriage over from the shipper, and must be entitled to believe that the bill of lading accurately sets out the terms and conditions of that contract.

Bill of lading as a receipt

When the ship arrives at the port of destination the shipowner will be obliged to let the person who holds the bill of lading take the goods. The bill of lading therefore acts as a receipt in that it describes the goods which have been loaded and which the holder is entitled to take. The Hague-Visby Rules govern most international sales contracts. These Rules require the bill of lading to show the "leading marks", which will enable the goods to be identified, the quantity of goods which have been shipped, the apparent order and condition of the goods loaded on board and the date on which the goods were loaded.

When the bill is a **clean bill of lading** then the shipowner acknowledges that the correct quantity of goods have been loaded on board and that these are in **apparent** good order and condition. The shipowner does not guarantee that the goods are in good order and condition but only that they appear to be. For example, if the goods loaded were Japanese televisions the shipowner could not reasonably be expected to guarantee that they were all of satisfactory quality. Instead, by issuing a clean bill he is only saying that they appear to be in good order and condition and that the correct quantity appear to have been loaded. If the goods did not appear to be in good order and condition the shipowner would issue a **claused or dirty bill** of lading. This would describe the way in which the goods did not appear to be in good order and condition. So, if for example the boxes containing the goods were waterlogged, the shipowner would issue a claused bill of lading which would say that they were. The shipowner must take great care not to issue a clean bill if the goods are not in apparent good order and condition. As between the seller and the shipowner the bill is prima facie evidence of the apparent order and condition of the goods. So it would be very difficult for the shipowner to argue with it. Once the bill of lading is transferred to a third party, it becomes **conclusive** evidence of the apparent order and condition of the goods when loaded. It would therefore be impossible to argue with it. A "shipped" bill says that the goods have been loaded on board a particular ship. A "received for shipment" bill merely says that the shipowner has received possession of the goods.

Bill of lading as a document of title

A bill of lading is a document of title and this means that the shipowner should allow the holder of the bill to take the goods from the ship. Mustill LJ in *Enichem Anic Spa v Ampelos Shipping Co Ltd* [1990] described the bill as a "transferable key to the warehouse". It is important to remember that the bill of lading's status as a document of title does not mean that whoever holds the bill owns the goods. Ownership of the goods will pass according to the rules set out in ss.16–20 SGA, as we shall see when considering FOB and CIF contracts below.

(FOB) FREE ON BOARD CONTRACTS

When goods are sold FOB the seller agrees to deliver the goods on board a nominated ship at a nominated port. Such sales are not necessarily international sales, although they usually are. Having delivered the goods on board, the seller has completed his obligations under the contract. The goods are then at the buyer's risk.

The duties of the parties

Devlin J identified three different types of FOB contracts in *Pyrene & Co Ltd v Scindia Steam Navigation Co Ltd* [1954]. In the **"classic" FOB** contract the buyer nominates the ship to be used and the seller makes the contract of carriage. After loading the goods on board the seller is given a bill of lading which he sends to the buyer. The buyer thereby gets constructive possession of the goods, and so he can collect them when the ship arrives at the port of destination. Under a **"FOB with additional services"** contract the seller again delivers goods on board a ship nominated by the buyer. The bill of lading is made out in the seller's name and this means that the seller is presumed to be reserving title to the goods until he has been fully paid for them. (SGA 1979 s.19(2).) The seller arranges and makes the contract of carriage and might also undertake to provide additional services such as insuring the goods. Under a **"FOB buyer contracting with carrier"** it is the buyer who makes the contract of carriage. When the seller puts the goods on board he gets a mate's receipt rather than a bill of lading. This is sent to the buyer and enables him to get a bill of lading. Whichever type of FOB contract is made, the seller delivers the goods by loading them on board the ship and it is the seller's duty to pay the loading costs.

Under two of Devlin LJ's three different types of FOB it is the seller who makes the contract of carriage. Once the buyer gets the bill of lading the buyer takes over the contract of carriage. If the shipowner negligently damages the goods it is the buyer who will want to sue. An obvious problem of privity arises, because the buyer wants to sue on a contract made by the seller. This problem is solved by s.2(1) Carriage of Goods by Sea Act 1992, which provides that the lawful holder of the bill of lading can sue on the contract of carriage as if he had made it.

Section 32(2) SGA 1979 requires that the seller make a reasonable contract of carriage, having regard to the nature of the goods and all the other circumstances. So, for example, if the goods were frozen a refrigerated ship would have to be booked. If the seller fails in this duty the buyer can either sue the seller for damages or claim that delivery to the carrier is not delivery of the goods to the buyer. The goods would therefore remain at the seller's risk after delivery to the carrier.

Nominating a ship

Unless the parties have agreed otherwise, the buyer must nominate the ship (name the ship to be used) and choose the port and the date of shipment. The ship nominated must be an 'effective' ship, meaning that it must be capable of carrying the goods and available to be booked to do so. If the ship nominated by the buyer cannot arrive in time, then the buyer is allowed to nominate another ship as long as it will arrive in time for the goods to be loaded within the contract period. If the buyer fails to nominate a ship which arrives in time for the seller to load the goods on board within the contract period, then the seller can treat the contract as repudiated. (*Bunge & Co Ltd v Tradax England Ltd* [1975].) Once the buyer has nominated the ship, and informed the seller of the nomination, the seller has a duty to load the goods on board that ship within the contract period. Failure to do this would be breach of a condition and so it would allow the buyer to treat the contract as repudiated.

Example

Harry sells goods to John FOB Hull for October shipment. This means that Harry must load the goods on board the nominated ship at Hull during the month of October. The ship which John nominates arrives in Hull on October 30. The sellers begin loading but do not get the goods on board by the end of the working day on October 31. If the failure to load was due to John not nominating a ship to arrive in time to allow the sellers to load, Harry can treat the contract as repudiated and sue for damages for non-acceptance under s.53. If the nominated ship did arrive in time to allow the sellers to load, Harry will have breached a condition by not loading within the contract period. John could therefore treat the contract as repudiated and sue for damages for non delivery under s.51.Whether or not the ship arrived in time to allow loading within the contract period would be a matter of fact to be decided by the court in the light of all the evidence.

Statutory implied terms

If the contract is governed by English law, then s.13 SGA 1979 will imply a condition that the goods correspond to any description by which they were sold. Section 14 will require the goods to be of satisfactory quality and fit for the buyer's purpose. In domestic sales goods must be of satisfactory quality at the time when the risk passes to the buyer. In FOB contracts risk passes when the goods go on board the ship. However, the goods have to remain of satisfactory quality in both FOB and CIF contracts until the goods arrive and are disposed of on arrival. (*Mash & Murrell Ltd v Joseph I Emanuel Ltd* [1961].)

The passing of the property and the risk

Section 17 SGA provides that the property will pass to the buyer at the time when the parties agree that it should. In an FOB contract the seller might reserve title until full payment, or the parties might agree that the property should pass at some time or other. If the seller takes the bill of lading in his own name then it is presumed that he is reserving title until full payment is made. If the parties to a FOB contract do not expressly agree when the property should pass, then it will pass when the goods cross the ship's rail. (Because the parties are taken to have intended this by making an FOB contract.) However, we saw in Ch.3 that property in unascertained goods cannot pass until the goods are ascertained. (Section 16 SGA.) So if unascertained goods are sold FOB and the buyer's goods have not been ascertained when the goods are loaded on board then the property cannot pass at this time. (The buyer might become a co-owner under s.20A, if all the requirements of that section are fulfilled, but that is a separate matter.) However, in an FOB contract **risk** will pass to the buyer as soon as the goods cross the ship's rail even if the property does not. Section 20(1) SGA provides that the risk passes with the property unless the parties have agreed otherwise, but by making an FOB contract the parties are taken to have agreed that the risk will pass on shipment even if the property has not yet passed. The buyer should therefore insure the goods from the moment when they cross the ship's rail. The effect of ss.16–20 were examined in Ch.3.

Section 33(3) SGA provides that where goods are sent from the seller to the buyer by a route involving sea transit, the seller must give the buyer notice which would enable the buyer to insure the goods. Such notice would need to include the name of the ship, particulars of the goods and the ports of departure and destination. (*Wimble v Rosenburg* [1913].) If the seller fails to give the buyer this notice then the goods remain at the seller's risk during the sea transit.

(CIF) COST, INSURANCE AND FREIGHT CONTRACTS

Unlike an FOB contract, a CIF contract is always an export contract. The contract names a port and this is the port at which the goods will arrive. The seller has to arrange the shipping contract with a shipowner, insure the goods and pay the freight (the cost of shipping). The seller must also deliver three documents to the buyer: a clean bill of lading; a policy of insurance; and an invoice for the goods. The buyer has the duty to accept and pay the contract price for the documents, if they are in order. If the documents presented are not in order then the buyer can reject them and treat the contract as repudiated. But if the documents are in order then the buyer must take and pay for them even if he knows that the goods have been lost. A buyer who fails to do this will have repudiated the contract. (*Manbre Sacharrine Co Ltd v Corn Products Ltd* [1919].)

Sellers like CIF contracts because they know that they will get paid for the documents, if they are in order. Buyers like such contracts because the sellers do all of the work, merely leaving the buyer the duty to pay the price. Buyers also like CIF because they can pledge the documents to a bank to raise money to finance the transaction.

The buyer must pay for the documents even if the goods themselves are not of satisfactory quality or do not match the description by which they were sold. However, the buyer could then reject the goods themselves when they arrive. (*Kwei Tek Chao v British Traders and Shippers Ltd* [1954].) The rule that the buyer **must** accept the documents and pay for them, if they are in order, seems to put buyers in an unenviable position. However, if the documents are in order the buyer will always be protected.

Example

Mary sells 100 tons of Kansas wheat to Neil CIF London. Mary presents Neil with the three necessary documents, all of which are in order. Neil must take and pay for the documents. If the wheat turns out not to be of satisfactory quality, when it arrives in London, Neil could reject the wheat itself and treat the contract as repudiated. If the wheat was damaged by the shipowner's negligence Neil, as the lawful holder of the bill of lading, could sue the shipowner on the contract of carriage. If the wheat was damaged otherwise than by the shipowner's negligence, Neil could sue on the contract of insurance. So in all eventualities Neil is afforded considerable protection. It is for this reason that the documents can be pledged to a bank to raise money. The bank knows that if the documents are in order they provide very good security.

Passing of the property and risk

In a domestic sale under which a seller sells specific goods in a deliverable state property will pass when the contract was

made. (Section 18 Rule 1.) When unascertained goods are sold
no property can pass until the goods are ascertained. (Section
16.) Property will then pass under s.18 Rule 5 when goods
matching the contract description and in a deliverable state are
unconditionally appropriated to the contract with the buyer's
assent. (These rules were considered in Ch.3.) When unascertained goods are sold CIF the seller must appropriate goods to
the contract, before or at the time of delivery of the documents,
so that the buyer is informed that it is only these goods which
the seller can tender. In a domestic sale this would pass
property to the buyer if the appropriation was unconditional.
However, in a CIF contract the parties are generally taken to
have shown an intention that the goods will pass when the
buyer takes and pays for the documents. (They might of course
expressly show a different intention.) As we have seen earlier, if
the bill of lading is taken out in the seller's name then the seller
is presumed to have reserved title until paid the full price. If the
buyer takes and pays for the documents before the goods have
become ascertained then (subject to s.20A) property cannot pass
to the buyer.

Risk will pass to the buyer from the time when the goods
were loaded on board the ship. This is the case even if, as
commonly happens, a buyer makes a CIF contract after the
goods have been loaded and after the ship has started the
voyage. Risk passes retrospectively because the documents give
the buyer continuous documentary cover, that is to say they
protect the buyer from the date on which the goods were loaded
on board.

Section 32(2) SGA will apply to CIF contracts and so the seller
must make a reasonable contract of carriage on the buyer's
behalf, as explained above in relation to FOB.

Other types of International Sales contracts

Ex-ship contracts

Under these contracts the seller must deliver the goods from a
ship which has reached the port of delivery. If the seller fails in
this duty then this amounts to a total failure of consideration,
and so the buyer can recover any of the price which has been
paid and sue for damages for non-delivery. In most ex-ship
contracts both property and risk pass on delivery.

Ex-works and ex-store contracts

These contracts may or may not be international sales contracts. The buyer has the obligation to collect the goods from the seller's works or stores. Property and risk usually passes upon delivery because the goods are usually unascertained goods.

8. THE AUTHORITY OF THE AGENT

THE NATURE OF AGENCY

An agent has the power to alter the legal position of another person, known as the principal. The most significant way in which an agent does this is by making contracts on behalf of the principal. However, agents can also affect the principal's legal position in other ways. For example, if money owed to a principal is paid to an agent, who has authority to take it on the principal's behalf, then the money is regarded as having been paid to the principal.

The importance of agency

Without agency the modern commercial world could not operate. If there was no such concept as agency, then only the owner of a business could make contracts on behalf of the business. Furthermore, there could be no companies or partnerships. Companies are legal persons but they are not human. They can operate only through human beings, and when these human beings alter the legal position of the company they do so as agents. Partners are agents of each other, and of the firm, for contracts made in the ordinary course of the firm's business. If partners were not agents in this way then partnership could not exist. Even sole traders commonly use agents to buy and sell, and otherwise run their businesses.

The parties involved in agency

We have seen that agents act on behalf of principals. When they alter a principal's legal position they do so in respect of third parties. It is convenient to refer to the three parties as A, P and T. For example, if an agent buys a car from a third party on behalf of the principal, we can say that A bought a car from T for P. The following diagram shows how agency operates when an agent with actual authority makes a contract with a third party on the principal's behalf.

Figure 1

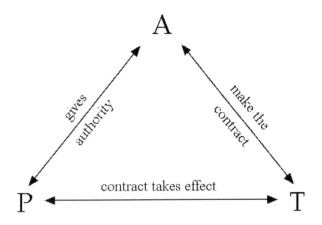

Employees and agency

Many employees are also agents. For example, shop assistants
are agents of the shop owners for whom they work and they are
also, almost always, employees of the shop owners. They are
agents because they sell goods belonging not to themselves but
to their principals (the shop owners). However, there is no
requirement that an agent is an employee of the principal and in
many cases they are not. For example, if I use a solicitor to sell
my house, the solicitor will be my agent but will not be my
employee. Some confusion can arise because it would be per-
fectly correct to say that I employed the agent to sell my house.
It is important to realise that **in this context the word employ is
not used in an employment law sense**. When a principal uses
the services of an agent he is said to employ that agent. This
does not necessarily mean that the agent is an employee of the
principal.

Mercantile agents

In Ch.4 we saw that the Factors Act 1889 allows a mercantile
agent to pass a good title to another person's goods, even when
he has no authority from that person to do this. This type of
agency is a special statutory agency and, as we saw in Ch.4, can
arise only if several conditions are satisfied.

Self-employed commercial agents

The Commercial Agents (Council Directive) Regulations 1993 have introduced the concept of a self-employed commercial agent. The Regs are highly technical, and they are important mainly when the employment of a self-employed commercial agent ends. They are therefore considered in Ch.10, which deals with termination of agency.

THE AUTHORITY OF AN AGENT

An agent cannot alter the legal position of a principal without authority to do so. There are two main types of authority, actual and apparent.

Actual authority

Actual authority is conferred on an agent when the principal and the agent agree that the agent should have the authority. This actual authority will enable the agent to alter the principal's legal position in respect of third parties. However, these third parties do not have a part to play in creating the authority, and do not even need to know that the agency exists. Actual authority is created solely by agreement between principal and agent.

Example

P asks A to sell his car for £1,000. A sells the car to T for £1,000. The contract of sale takes effect between P and T. P and A agreed with each other that A should have the authority to make this contract, and so A had actual authority to make it. This actual authority arose quite independently of any actions of T.

Express and implied actual authority

We have seen that actual authority arises when P and A agree that A should have the authority. If this agreement is made in words, then this is known as **express actual authority**. It does not matter whether the words were written or spoken. If the agreement was made otherwise than in words, the agent will have **implied actual authority**. Express actual authority and implied actual authority are both types of actual authority. Therefore the effect of the actual authority will be the same, regardless of which way it arose. It will enable the agent to make contracts which bind the principal, as long as these were made within the scope of the authority. It is vital to remember that the distinction between express actual authority and implied actual authority is concerned with **how** the actual authority arose. Whether the authority arose as express actual or implied actual authority, it arose because P agreed that A should have the authority and either way A can therefore create a contract between P and T, as long as A acts within the actual authority.

It is relatively easy to decide the scope of express actual authority. The authority was conferred expressly, in words, and so all that has to be decided is whether or not the agent acted within the authority conferred by those words. For example, if in the example above, A had sold P's car for £900 he would not have had actual authority to do so. The express words made it plain that the car was not to be sold for less than £1,000.

The scope of implied actual authority is less easy to determine. A court must decide whether the principal and agent agreed, otherwise than in words, that the agent should do the act in question. Lord Denning MR illustrated the difference in *Hely-Hutchinson v Brayhead Ltd* [1968]. He said that a board of directors might expressly agree that two directors had authority to sign cheques on behalf of the company. These two directors would therefore have express actual authority to sign the cheques. But if the board of directors of a company appointed a person managing director, they would give him implied actual authority to do all of the things which the managing director of such a company would normally do. (Because they would agree with that person that he would have this authority.)

Implied actual authority will very commonly amplify and extend express actual authority.

Example

P, who owns a bicycle shop, appoints A as shop assistant and tells A to try his hardest to sell one particular bicycle. A will have express actual authority to sell that particular bicycle because he was expressly told to do so. He will have implied actual authority to sell all the other bicycles because, in giving him the job, P impliedly told A to do so. Either way A has actual authority to sell the bicycles.

Implied actual authority cannot override an express prohibition. For example, in *Waugh v Clifford* [1982] solicitors (A) were told by P not to settle a legal case on terms which had been suggested to A by T. Nevertheless, A did settle on these terms. As A had been expressly told not to settle on these terms, it was not possible for A to argue that they had implied actual authority to do so.

If the extent of actual authority is ambiguous, an agent who acts reasonably believing that he is within the instructions will have actual authority. (*Ireland v Livinston* [1871].)

Ratification

A principal who ratifies a contract, made by an agent who had no actual authority to make the contract, later agrees to be bound by it. This is therefore regarded as a form of actual authority. P did agree to authorise what the agent did, but the authorisation was given retrospectively.

However, ratification is possible only if the following conditions are satisfied. First, the agent must have purported to have acted as an agent, and the identity of the principal on whose behalf he acted must have been capable of being ascertained by the third party at the time of the contract. Second, the principal must have been in existence at the time of the contract. Third, the principal must have been aware of all the material facts at the time of ratification or have intended to ratify no mater what the facts might be. Fourth, the principal must have had the legal capacity to make the contract, both when the agent made it and when the principal ratified it. Fifth, a void act cannot be ratified. If these conditions are satisfied, the contract is regarded as binding on the principal and the third party from the date on which the agent made the contract. This is because the agent is regarded as having had actual authority at that time.

Example

A has actual authority from P to buy potatoes to the value of £5,000 from T but not to go any higher. On Monday A buys potatoes to the value of £6,000 from T, saying that he is acting for P. At this stage there is no actual authority for A to buy the potatoes as he was told not to pay more than £5,000. On Wednesday P ratifies the contract. A contract now exists between P and T, under which P has bought the potatoes for

£6,000. Furthermore, this contract takes affect from the time when A made the contract on Monday, just as if A had been given prior actual authority to make the contract.

The retrospective nature of ratification was confirmed in *Bolton Partners v Lambert* [1889]. In the case T tried to revoke an offer which A (without authority) had accepted on P's behalf. After T tried to revoke the offer, P ratified A's acceptance. It was held that T could not revoke his offer. P's ratification was retrospectively effective, and so A had actual authority to accept T's offer on the date on which he did accept it. However, ratification will not have retroactive effect if the contract between A and T was made "subject to ratification", or if the retroactive effect would interfere with a third party's property rights which had arisen before ratification, or if the ratification was not made within a reasonable time.

Consequences of A having actual authority

If an agent acting with actual authority creates a contract on the principal's behalf with a third party, the consequences will be as follows. First, a contract will exist between P and T and either P or T can enforce this contract. Second, A will have no liability to either P or T. Third, if A was to be paid commission by P for making the contract, A will be entitled to this commission.

Apparent (or ostensible) authority

Apparent authority does not arise because P and A have agreed that A should have authority. It arises because P makes a representation to T that A has authority and, having made such a representation, P is estopped from denying it. It is the authority of A as it appears to T. The three requirements for apparent authority to exist are as follows. First, P must have made a representation to T that A had authority. Second, the representation must have been made by P, or by someone to whom P had given authority to make it. Third, the third party must have relied on the representation. If apparent authority existed when A made the contract P will be estopped from denying that A had the authority to make it.

An agent commonly has both apparent authority and actual authority to make the same contract. In *Hely-Hutchinson v Brayhead Ltd* [1968] Lord Denning illustrated this. We have already seen that he said that if the board of directors appoint an agent to be managing director they thereby give the agent implied actual authority to make whatever contracts a managing director of such a company would usually make. (Because they impliedly agreed with the agent that he should make these contracts.) Lord Denning then went on to say that the board of directors would also have given the managing director apparent authority to make the kind of contracts which the managing director of such a company would usually make. This apparent authority would have been created because the three necessary steps would have been taken. First, by appointing A as managing director, P would have made a representation to people dealing with the company (Ts) that A could make the kind of contracts which a managing director of such a company would usually make. Second, this representation was made by the board of directors and P (the company) would have given the board actual authority (in the articles of association) to exercise all of P's powers and thus to make the representation. Third, a person (T) contracting with the company, through the managing director, would have relied on the representation by making the contract with the company.

As the managing director would already have had actual authority to make a contract on behalf of P with T, it would generally make little difference that he also had apparent authority to do so. However, apparent authority would become important if P, unknown to T, had limited A's authority. To illustrate this, Lord Denning extended his example. He said that if the board of directors, when appointing A as managing director, had told A that he was not to make contracts worth more than £500, A could not have actual authority to make such contracts. But if A ignored this instruction and did make a contract worth more than £500 with T, on behalf of P, then P would be bound by the contract because A would have had apparent authority to make it.

The consequences of A having apparent authority

The consequences of an agent having apparent authority are not the same as his having actual authority. The consequences are as follows. First, T can enforce the contract against P, because P is estopped from denying the representation which he made. Second, P cannot enforce the contract against T, because T made no representation. (However, if T does choose to enforce the contract, P can then insist that T performs his side of the bargain.) Third, if the enforcement of the contract causes loss to P, P can sue A for damages for causing this loss while acting outside his actual authority. If P is able to ratify the contract then actual authority would be retrospectively conferred, and these last two consequences would be changed. Having ratified, P could then enforce the contract against T and P could not sue A for damages. (Because A would be regarded as having had actual authority when he made the contract.)

Waugh v HB Clifford & Sons Ltd [1982] neatly illustrates the different effects of actual and apparent authority. P (a firm of builders) were threatened with legal action by T. P employed A, (a firm of solicitors,) to deal with the matter. A suggested to P that they should settle the action in a certain way. P told A not to do this. Nevertheless A went ahead and did settle in this way. T claimed that the settlement was binding on P. The settlement was held to be binding on P, because A had apparent authority to make the settlement. Furthermore, as A had no actual authority to settle in the way in which they did, they would be liable to P for any loss which this caused to P. If A had had actual authority to settle the action, then it would still be the case that T could have insisted that the settlement was binding. However, A would not have had to pay damages to P. Furthermore, P could also have insisted that the settlement was binding if T had not wanted to be bound by it.

The main difficulty with apparent authority is in deciding exactly what it is that P has represented to T. We have seen from Lord Denning's example in *Hely-Hutchinson* that if P appoints A to a certain position then this amounts to a representation that A can make the type of contracts which a person in that position could usually make. To use another example, if A is made a shop assistant then P is representing to customers that A can sell the shop's stock, as this is what a shop assistant would usually do. However, If T either knows or ought to know that A cannot do a certain thing then A will not have apparent authority to do that thing. (*ArmagasLtd v Mundogas SA* [1985].) Nor will apparent authority exist unless the representation came from P, or from someone to whom P had given actual or apparent authority to make it. So when P appoints A to a position it can be difficult to decide exactly what P has represented by doing this. *First Energy Ltd v Hungarian International Bank Ltd* [1993] considered this problem. P, a bank, appointed A to the position of senior manager of its Manchester office. A told

T that he (A) did not have the power to grant a loan, that only head office had this power. Later A told T that head office had granted a loan to T. T relied on this. Later still it came to light that A had been mistaken, and that head office had not granted the loan. The Court of Appeal held that A did have apparent authority to communicate the decisions of head office. By appointing A as senior manager, P had represented to T that A had this authority. If A had told T that he himself (A) was granting the loan then there could have been no apparent authority as T knew that A did not have the authority to do this.

Exam Tip: Do not start by considering apparent authority until you have considered actual authority. If an agent had actual authority then there will generally be no need to consider whether he also had apparent authority.

A separate category of "usual authority"?

The term "usual authority" is one which must be used with great care. It can be used in several different ways. First, it can be used as a **type of implied actual authority**. We have already seen that when a principal appoints an agent to a certain position, then they both agree that the agent should have the authority which would usually be given to a person in such a position. The agent therefore has implied actual authority to do what a person in such a position would usually do.

Second, "usual authority" can be a **type of apparent authority**. When a principal appoints an agent to a certain position, we have seen that he gives the agent apparent authority to do what an agent in such a position would usually do. This apparent authority arose because, as we have seen, the principal represented to third parties that the agent had the authority.

Third, usual authority can be used to describe the **type of authority conferred in *Watteau v Fenwick* [1893]**. In that case P, the owner of a pub, gave A authority to manage the pub. However, P told A not to buy tobacco on credit. A's name remained above the pub door, because A had owned the pub until he had sold it to P. T sold A tobacco on credit, thinking that A was the owner of the pub. P refused to be bound by the contract. Wills J held that the manager had 'usual authority' to make the contract and so P was bound by it.

Exam Tip: *Watteau v Fenwick* is a troublesome case. The best approach to it is first to explain why there was no actual authority. (Because A had been forbidden to buy tobacco on credit.) Second, to explain why there was no apparent authority. (Because T, the tobacco salesman, could not say that P made a representation to him, to the effect that A had authority, if he did not even know that P existed or that A was an agent.) Third, to apply the decision cautiously, aware that it has been much criticised. The case is applicable if the following two conditions are satisfied. First, T does not know that A is an agent; and second, A does an act which he has no actual authority to do, but which an agent in his position would usually have authority to do.

Criticism of the case

There is some doubt as to whether or not *Watteau v Fenwick* would be followed. Canadian courts have refused to follow it but there is no record of an English court either following it or not following it. It certainly seems strange that T could sue P on the contract when neither T nor P intended to contract with each other. It also seems strange that P should be liable on the contract to T, but have no opportunity to enforce it against T. (Ratification would not be possible because A did not purport to act for an ascertainable principal.)

Agency by operation of law

Some statutes, such as the Consumer Credit Act 1974, can create a **statutory agency**. These agencies operate outside normal principles on an agent's authority, and are best ignored unless studying the relevant statutory sections.

Agency can arise through **cohabitation**. If a couple live together it is possible that one will have the authority to buy necessary goods and services using the credit of the other. However, this is of very little importance in commercial law.

An **agency of necessity** can arise if a person in control of another's property is faced with a commercial emergency, and finds it impossible to get that person's instructions. This type of authority grew out of cases involving ship's captains who were either forced to sell the principal's goods when they were damaged by the sea or were forced to repair the ship when it became damaged. As long as the captain could not possibly get instructions in time from the principal, and as long as he acted in good faith, an agency of necessity was created. Agency of necessity has declined in importance as modern methods of communication have greatly reduced the circumstances in which an agent cannot communicate with the principal.

---

9. RIGHTS AND LIABILITIES OF THE PRINCIPAL, AGENT AND THIRD PARTY

THE PRINCIPAL'S RIGHTS AND LIABILITIES ON THE CONTRACT CREATED BY THE AGENT

Disclosed and undisclosed agency distinguished

Agency is **undisclosed** where the third party does not know that the agent is acting as an agent. Agency is **disclosed** where the third party does know that the agent is acting as an agent, even if he does not know the identity of the principal.

Disclosed agency

If the agent had **actual authority** to make the contract for a disclosed principal, then P can enforce the contract against T, and T can enforce the contract against P. The position is the same as if P had made the contract himself.

We saw in the previous chapter that if a principal **ratifies** a contract made by an agent acting without prior actual authority, ratification is regarded as retrospective actual authority. So after an effective ratification P can enforce the contract against T and T can enforce it against P, just as if the agent had had actual authority when he made the contract. You should however remember the limits on ratification, (see Ch.8), particularly that ratification cannot be effective unless the agent acted on behalf of an ascertainable principal. So ratification will not be possible if the agency was undisclosed. Nor will it be possible if the agency was disclosed, so that T at least knows that A was acting as an agent, but T could not have identified who the principal was.

If the agent had **apparent authority**, but no actual authority, then P cannot enforce the contract against T (unless ratification is possible and effected by P). T can however enforce the contract against P, and if T does this P can of course counterclaim for T's consideration. In the *Watteau v Fenwick* situation P cannot choose to enforce the contract against T because A had no actual or apparent authority and made the contract in his own name, thus making ratification impossible. However, T can enforce the contract against P, and if T does this P can counterclaim T's consideration.

The doctrine of the undisclosed principal

The doctrine of the undisclosed principal allows P to sue T on the contract, even though T did not know that A was acting for a principal. The doctrine is justified on the grounds of commercial convenience. (*Keighley Maxted & Co. Durant* [1901].) However, the agent must have had **prior actual authority** to make the contract. (This is why *Watteau v Fenwick* was **not** an example of the doctrine of the undisclosed principal.)

Despite the doctrine of the undisclosed principal, there are three circumstances in which a principal cannot sue on a contract made by an undisclosed agent.

First, where a **term of the contract excluded agency**. For example, in *Humble v Hunter* [1848] an undisclosed agent chartered a ship to T but the agent's mother, the owner of the ship, could not sue on the contract as an undisclosed principal. When making the contract the agent had described himself as owner of the ship, and so he had impliedly stated that there was no undisclosed principal.

Second, in some circumstances, where **the third party would have refused to have contracted with the undisclosed principal**. The most famous example of this is *Said v Butt* [1920]. P was banned from T's theatre. He wanted to attend the opening night of a play so he asked A to buy him a ticket without revealing that he was acting for P. A bought the ticket, but T would not let P into the theatre. It was held that P had no right to enforce the contract as T would not have contracted with P and "*the personal element was strikingly present*". If the contract in *Said v Butt* had been to buy generic goods then the exception would not have applied, as the personal element would not have been strikingly present. However, even when buying generic goods or land, if A tells T that he is not acting for a certain person that person cannot later intervene as an undisclosed principal. (*Archer v Stone* [1898].)

Third, an undisclosed principal will not be allowed to intervene **where the third party relied on the agent's personal qualities**. For example, if a famous singer, A, made a contract to sing at T's theatre, it would not be permissible for another singer, P, to say that the famous singer made the contract on his behalf.

THE THIRD PARTY'S RIGHTS AND LIABILITIES ON THE CONTRACT CREATED BY THE AGENT

Disclosed agency

If a disclosed agent acted with **actual authority** then T can sue P, and be sued by P, on the contract. (And if there is an affective **ratification** this is regarded as retrospective actual authority.) If the agent acted with **apparent, but not actual, authority** then T can sue P on the contract, even though P cannot choose to enforce the contract. (Because P made a representation to T, but T made no representation to P.) A disclosed agent will not be liable to T on a contract made on P's behalf. However, A might be liable for breach of warranty of authority, a matter which is considered below.

It is possible for an agent to contract with T on the terms that both he (A) and P will be jointly liable on the contract. If this is done then T can choose to sue either A or P on the contract. However, once T has **unequivocally elected** to hold either A or P liable on the contract T will not be able to change his mind and sue the other.

Generally a third party who **settles with an agent** who is acting on behalf of a disclosed principal will not be regarded as having settled with the principal. But T will be regarded as having settled with P if A had either actual or apparent authority to take the money on P's behalf. So a third party who pays a shop assistant for goods bought is regarded as having settled with the shop owner. The shop assistant (A) certainly has apparent authority, and almost always has actual authority, to take T's money on P's behalf.

Undisclosed agency

Where an agent acts for an **undisclosed principal** T can sue the agent on the contract from the moment when it was created. Once the undisclosed principal is revealed, T can sue **either** P or A on the contract. This choice will cease to exist only when T has **unequivocally elected** to sue either A or P. Having made such an unequivocal election, T will be stuck with it. In *Clarkson Booker Ltd v Andjel* [1964] the Court of Appeal held that, on the facts of the case, even issuing a writ against the undisclosed principal was not enough to amount to an unequivocal election by T to hold P, rather than A, liable on the contract. T could therefore still sue A on the contract.

Where an agent makes a contract on behalf of an undisclosed principal, T can **set off** against P any defences and rights which already existed against A. This is because T thought that he was making the contract with A. For example, A owes T £10,000. A makes a contract with T, on behalf of an undisclosed principal. Under the contract A sold P's stock of wheat to T for £25,000. T can set the existing debt off against P, and therefore need pay P only £15,000. P could claim the other £10,000 from A.

If the **third party settles with an undisclosed agent** then this is regarded as settling with P, even if A does not hand the money over to P. For example, T buys a car for £5,000 from A who is selling on behalf of an undisclosed principal. T pays A the full price but A disappears with the money. T is regarded as having paid the money to P and therefore had no further obligation to pay. Both the right of set-off and the rule that settlement with the agent is settlement with the undisclosed principal are regarded as a form of estoppel. By allowing an undisclosed agent to act for him, P has represented that T can settle with A or set off rights and duties which existed against A. However, it can be argued that estoppel is an inappropriate explanation, because it is difficult to see how an undisclosed principal can make representations to a third party who does not know of his existence.

THE AGENT'S RIGHTS AGAINST AND LIABILITIES TO THE THIRD PARTY

Disclosed agency

Generally, if the agency is **disclosed** the agent can neither sue on the contract created with T, nor be sued on it, as it was not his contract. (*Montgomerie v United Kingdom Mutual Steamship Association* [1891].) There are exceptions to this rule, the most important one being that either the contract or the surrounding circumstances might indicate that A is incurring personal liability, as well as making P liable.

Undisclosed agency

If the agency is **undisclosed** then initially it is the agent who is liable to T on the contract (because T thought that the contract was being made with A). But when the undisclosed principal is revealed then P **also** becomes liable on the contract. This liability of P does not automatically absolve A from liability. Both parties remain liable on the contract and T can choose which one of them to sue if the contract is not performed. Only where T has made an **unequivocal election** to sue either A or P will he be prevented from changing his mind and suing the other one. In *Clarkson Booker Ltd v Andjel* [1964] it was held that even issuing a writ against P was not enough to amount to an unequivocal election to hold P liable on the contract.

Other ways in which the agent can incur contractual liability

There are two other ways in which the agent might incur contractual liability. The important thing to remember here is that both of these types of contractual liability do not arise out of the contract which A created with T on P's behalf. They arise as a separate contract with either T or P.

First, an agent might be liable to T for **breach of warranty of authority**. This liability arises if an agent claims to have authority when he does not in fact have it, and if T relies on this claim and thereby suffers a loss. A is regarded as having warranted his authority, and if this warranty is breached then A is liable for breach of warranty. For example, in *Yonge v Toynbee* [1910] A (a solicitor) claimed to have authority to act for P (a client) after this authority had been revoked. This claim led T, to whom the claim was made, to incur legal costs. A was liable to T for these costs. Three point should be noted. First, liability is strict (being for breach of contract) and it was no defence that the solicitor did not know that his authority had been revoked. Second, damages were assessed under general contract principles according to *Hadley v Baxendale* [1854]. Third, there will be no liability if the third party knows that the agent did not have the authority which he claimed to have.

The second way in which an agent might be contractually liable is for breaching a duty which he owed to the principal. (This matter is considered immediately below, under the heading "Contractual duties".)

THE DUTIES WHICH THE AGENT OWES TO THE PRINCIPAL

Agents owe both contractual and fiduciary duties to their principals.

Contractual duties

Three contractual duties are owed by an agent to the principal: to obey instructions; to use an appropriate amount of care and skill; and to perform the agency duties personally.

To obey instructions

An agent has a duty to obey the instructions given to him. Failure to obey these instructions can make the agent liable to the principal. For example, in *Turpin v Bilton* [1843] A undertook to insure P's ship. Despite having had ample opportunity to do so, A failed to insure the ship. When the ship was lost, A was liable to P for having failed to obey his instructions. Generally, the duty to obey instructions arises out of a bilateral contract between A and P. P usually agrees to pay A, and in return A agrees to do what he has been instructed to do. If the contract between A and P is unilateral, then A will not have promised to do anything and therefore will not be liable if he fails to do what he was asked to do. For example, If P said to A "If you sell my car I will pay you £1,000" then A has no contractual duty to sell the car. A **gratuitous agent** acts for no reward and so there is no contract between A and P. (P has provided no consideration.) So a gratuitous agent will not be contractually liable for failing to do what he agreed to do. (He may however be liable in tort if he breaches a duty of care owed to P.)

Duty to use reasonable care and skill

Both in contract and in tort, an agent has a duty to use reasonable care and skill. The standard required will depend upon all of the circumstances. Agents who act in a professional capacity will be expected to show the level of care and skill which a reasonably competent member of that profession would show.

When a service is provided in the course of a business, the term as to reasonable care and skill is required by s.13 of the Supply of Goods and Services Act 1982, which was considered in Ch.2. (The Act does not apply to services provided in the course of employment.) Gratuitous agents also owe a duty to use reasonable care and skill. This duty arises in tort rather than in contract. (*Chaudry v Prabhakar* [1988].) A contractual term might attempt to limit or exclude the duty to use reasonable care and skill. However, such a term would be subject to s.2 of the Unfair Contract Terms Act 1977 as this act would regard breach of the duty as "negligence". So a term which tried to exclude liability for death or personal injury caused by negligence would be rendered completely ineffective. A term which tried to restrict or exclude other types of loss caused by negligence would be subject to the Act's requirement of reasonableness. The UCTA definition of negligence includes the breach of a contractual duty to exercise reasonable skill in the performance of a contract. Section 2 UCTA was considered in slightly more detail in Ch.2.

Duty to perform personally

Generally, an agent is under a duty to perform his duties personally. However, delegation to a sub-agent is allowed if the principal expressly or impliedly authorises it. It is also allowed if the duty which is delegated is purely ministerial, that is to say it is a duty which requires no skill or competence.

If an agent does make an unauthorised delegation to a sub-agent, the principal will not be bound by what the sub-agent does, (unless the agent was given apparent authority to delegate). So the agent will be liable to the principal for having exceeded his authority and the principal will not have to pay to the sub-agent any commission which was to be paid to the agent. In *Henderson v Merritt Syndicates Ltd* [1994] the House of Lords held that a sub-agent who owed a duty of care to a principal could be liable to the principal in the tort of negligence, even if there was no privity of contract. (However, this would depend upon their being a relationship which was sufficiently proximate between P and the sub-agent.) They also decided that this liability could extend to mere economic loss.

Fiduciary duties

The fiduciary duties which an agent owes to his principal are: to avoid a conflict of interest; not to make a secret profit; not to take a bribe; the duty to account and the duty to preserve confidentiality. These duties overlap to some extent but they are more easily understood if considered separately.

The duty to avoid a conflict of interest

In *Aberdeen Railway v Blaikie Bros* [1854] Lord Cranworth gave the classic description of this duty: "*It is a rule of universal application that no-one having [fiduciary] duties to discharge, should be allowed to enter into engagements in which he has, or can have, a personal interest conflicting, or which may possibly conflict, with the interests of those whom he is bound to protect.*" Notice that it is not enough to avoid an actual conflict of interest, an agent should not allow even a possible conflict between his own interests and those of the principal. However, A conflict of interest is allowed if it is agreed upon by the principal.

Bentley v Craven [1853] provides an example of an agent being liable for a conflict of interest. The agent in question, C, was in partnership with two others, A and B, as sugar refiners. All partners are agents of all other partners for the purpose of the business of the partnership. (This rule has been given statutory effect by s.5 of the Partnership Act 1890.) A and B knew that C carried on business on his own account as a sugar dealer and they consented to this. C managed to buy some sugar very cheaply and sold it to the firm at the going wholesale rate. This created a conflict between C's interests and those of A and B. C therefore had to account to the firm for all the profit made on this transaction. Notice that C did not have to account to the firm for profits he made by generally buying and selling sugar, because the other partners agreed to his doing this on his own account.

The duty not to make a secret profit

In *Boardman v Phipps* [1965] Lord Denning MR said that an agent must not (without the principal's consent) use the principal's property to make a profit for himself. Nor must he use a position of authority conferred by the principal. Nor must he use information or knowledge which he has acquired for the use of the principal. This is a very broad statement of the agent's duty not to make a secret profit. When the case reached the House of Lords it was held that the agent, who had used information gained as a result of his agency, had to account for all the profit which he made by using that information. This was the case even though the same actions which caused the agent to make the profit also caused the principal to make a very good profit.

Any secret profit which the agent makes will have to be given to the principal. If it is not, it is possible that it may be held on constructive trust for the principal. So if the profit made increases in value the agent might have to account for this increased value as well as for the profit originally made.

The duty not to take a bribe

A bribe here has a much broader meaning that its usual meaning. Slade J in *Industries and General Mortgage Co. Ltd v*

Lewis [1949] said that a bribe meant a secret commission. A payment would be a bribe if it was made to an agent, knowing that the agent was acting for a principal, and if it was not disclosed to the principal. In *Boston Deep Sea Fishing and Ice Co. v Ansell* [1888] A, the managing director of a company, ordered two new boats for P, the company. The shipbuilders made a secret payment to A. This was held to be a bribe and A had to pay it, with interest, to P. Furthermore P was entitled to dismiss A.

The duty to account

This duty requires the agent to keep his own money and property separate from the principal's. Failure to do this might mean that the whole of the mixed property belongs to the principal. At the end of the agency the agent will have to hand over to the principal all documents and notes which relate to the principal's property. *Yasuda Ltd v Orion Underwriting Ltd* [1995] held that material stored on a computer could also be included. At any time, the agent will have to allow the principal to inspect documentation which relates to the agency.

The duty to preserve confidentiality

An agent has a duty to preserve the principal's confidentiality. So an agent must not disclose confidential information or documents to third parties. In *Bolkiah v KPMG* [1999] the House of Lords held that this was an absolute duty which went beyond merely taking reasonable precautions. This duty continues after the agency has been terminated.

Remedies for breach of fiduciary duties

It is not possible to state with certainty exactly what remedies will be available if an agent commits a breach of fiduciary duties. Where the breach causes the agent to make a profit, the following remedies might be available. Recover the profit made by the agent; dismiss the agent without notice; recover a bribe from either the agent or the person who paid it, or (alternatively) sue either the agent or the person paying the bribe for damages in respect of losses caused by the bribe; and rescind the contract with the third party.

It should be stressed that as it is a fiduciary duty which has been breached the court has considerable discretion in awarding remedies. If the breach is technical, rather than dishonest, the remedies will reflect this. For example, in *Hippisley v Knee* [1905] an auctioneer who was asked to sell goods and to advertise the auction committed a breach of fiduciary duty. He bought the advertising at trade rates but then charged the principal the non-trade rate which the principal would have had to pay if he had been buying the advertising. This was held to be a breach of the duty not to make a secret profit. The remedy was merely that the agent should account to the principal for the profit he had made on the advertising. As the agent had not acted fraudulently, he was entitled to keep the commission agreed in the contract.

By contract, in *Attorney-General for Hong Kong v Reid* [1994] the agent committed a serious, fraudulent, breach of duty. He was a customs officer and took large bribes. With the profits made from this the agent bought three properties. By the time of the trial these properties had increased greatly in value. The Privy Council held that these three properties were held in trust for the principal (the Crown). The principal could also dismiss the agent (who was in fact sentenced to over eight years imprisonment). But even in a case such as this, Lord Diplock made it plain that the right to recover the bribe and the right to sue for damages for fraud were alternative. A bribe could be recovered even if the principal had suffered no loss. But *"damage is the gist of an action in fraud"* so if the bribe was recovered this amount would have to be deducted from the amount of any damages, as it would reduce the loss suffered.

Duties owed by Commercial Agents

The Commercial Agents Regulations 1993 impose duties on both principals and agents. These Regs are of interest mainly in relation to termination of agency and so they are examined in the following chapter, where the definition of a commercial agent is set out. It should be noted that if an agent does not come within this definition then the Regs will not apply. The duties imposed are in addition to duties imposed by the common law.

Regulation 3(1) imposes duties to look after the interests of the principal and to act dutifully and in good faith. Regulation 3(2) says that in particular a commercial agent must: (a) make proper efforts to negotiate and, where appropriate, conclude the transactions he is instructed to take car of; (b) communicate to his principal all the necessary information available to him; and (c) comply with reasonable instructions given by his principal. These duties add little to the common law duties imposed on all agents, whether commercial agents or not. However, the duties are expressed as positive duties to be performed, whereas the common law duties are negative ones which must not be breached. It is not possible for the parties to contract out of the duties imposed by the Regulations. (Regulation 5(1).)

THE AGENT'S RIGHTS AGAINST THE PRINCIPAL

An agent might have a right to remuneration, to an indemnity or to a lien.

The right to remuneration

An agent will have a right to receive payment from the principal only if an express or implied term of the contract between P and A gives such a right. Express terms as to remuneration are interpreted in the same way as other contractual terms. That is to say, they are interpreted so as to give effect to the intentions of the parties. In *Re Richmond Gate Property Co Ltd* [1965] the agent's contract entitled him to *"such remuneration . . . as the directors may determine"*. By the time P (the company) went into liquidation the directors had not voted to pay A anything. A could not claim any salary. His contract with P set out his remuneration and there was no room for the court to ignore this and pay him on a *quantum meruit*.

If the contract is silent as to the amount of payment, and if the agent is not an employee, then s.15 of the Supply of Goods and Services Act 1982 will entitle the agent to receive a reasonable price for services provided while acting in the course of a business.

Where the agent is to be paid commission if he achieves some purpose, then it is possible that a term might be implied to prevent the principal from making the achievement of the purpose impossible. However, such a term was not implied by the House of Lords in *Luxor v Cooper* [1941]. It is difficult to know whether or not this case established a general principle. The case may have be restricted to its own facts. In the case the agents, estate agents, were to be paid a huge sum if they found a purchaser for a chain of cinemas. The commission was payable on completion. After A found a purchaser, P refused to complete the sale. It was held that the sum payable was so huge that the agents were regarded as having taken a chance that P would not complete. Most estate agents now contract on the basis that they will be paid their commission if they find a purchaser ready, willing and able to purchase the property.

An agent who acts outside his actual authority will not be entitled to remuneration. Furthermore, agents who commit a serious breach of duty or who act in an unlawful manner may lose the right to remuneration.

Indemnity

An indemnity is a payment made to compensate an agent for expenses incurred on the principal's behalf. For example, if P sends A an email telling A to travel to London to buy goods at an auction, A could claim an indemnity for his travel expenses. Such an indemnity might arise as either an express or implied term of the contract between P and A. However, if an express term of the contract states that an agent is not entitled to an indemnity then he will not be entitled to one. An implied term cannot overrule an express term. When an agent acts gratuitously there is no contract between P and A. Nevertheless, gratuitous agents can be entitled to claim an indemnity as a restitutionary right.

Lien

A lien is a self-help remedy. It entitles an agent who is owed money by a principal to retain possession of P's goods until the debt is paid. It does not give the agent ownership of such goods. As the agent's lien is a particular lien (rather than a general lien) it arises only over the particular goods in respect of which the money is owed.

There will be no right to a lien if the contract between P and A expressly or impliedly excludes such a right. Furthermore, the lien can be exercised only in respect of goods which have lawfully come into the agent's possession, in his capacity as agent, and which are still held in that way. Constructive possession is good enough. The right can be lost by waiving it, or by voluntarily surrendering possession of the goods.

LIABILITY IN TORT

If the agent is also an employee of the principal, then the principal will be vicariously liable for torts committed by the agent in the course of his employment. As regards agents who are not employees, a distinction must be made between torts committed by making an untrue representation and torts committed in other ways.

Untrue representations

If the tort is committed by the agent making an untrue representation to the third party then the principal can be liable either in the tort of deceit, or under s.2(1) Misrepresentation Act 1967, or under *Hedley Byrne v Heller and Partners* [1964]. T may also gain the right to rescind the contract made on P's behalf. However, this will be the case only if the agent had actual or apparent authority to make the statement.

Other torts

As regards torts committed otherwise than by making an untrue representation, the general rule is that the principal will be liable only if the agent had actual authority to commit the tort. If the principal ratifies the agent's tortious act then the agent will be regarded as having had actual authority. If the agent is also personally liable for the tort, then liability is joint and several, meaning that the third party can sue whichever party he chooses for the full amount. (The party who is sued may be able to recover a contribution from the other party who was liable, under The Civil Liability (Contribution) Act 1978.)

10. TERMINATION OF AGENCY

Withdrawal of authority

When we considered creation of agency, we saw that an agent can alter a principal's legal position only if he has some authority to do so. We saw also that the authority might be actual or apparent.

If a principal who has given an agent actual authority withdraws that authority, then the agent will no longer have actual authority to act for the principal. However, the agent might still be able to bind the principal to third parties on account of having apparent authority. Actual authority is created by agreement between P and A and so can (almost always) be withdrawn by P. Apparent authority arises because P makes a representation to T that A has the power to act for P. Even if P withdraws A's actual authority, apparent authority might still exist. For example, in *Trueman v Loder* [1840] P, a Russian, used A to carry out all of his business in London. P withdrew A's authority, but A sold goods to T who believed that A was acting for P. P was held liable on the contract. A's actual authority had ceased to exist but his apparent authority lived on because T had not received notice that A's authority had been terminated.

Except in cases of gratuitous agency, there will be a contract between P and A. If P withdraws A's authority in such a way that this contract is breached, then A will be able to sue P for breach of contract. However, the contract between A and P might already have been terminated, in which case A will not have a claim against P. For example, if the contract is to perform a one-off duty, and A duly performs the duty, then the contract between A and P will have been discharged by performance. In a similar way, if the contract was for a fixed time, and the time period has expired, the contract will again be discharged by performance. A contract which was to exist for a fixed time might be ended early if both parties agree to this. It will then have been discharged by agreement. But if a contract was stated to be for a fixed term and either A or P unilaterally terminates it early, then this will be a breach of contract and the innocent party will be entitled to damages. (If an agent who is an employee is dismissed without notice then there might also be a claim for unfair dismissal. Such a claim is statutory and is explained in *Nutshell on Employment Law*.)

If the contract of agency becomes illegal or impossible to perform then it will be discharged by frustration. (*Morgan v Manser* [1948].) If the agent commits a repudiatory breach of contract then the principal will be entitled to dismiss him without notice.

The principles stated above, relating to discharge of the contract between A and P, are no more than the general principles which apply to discharge of contracts. A contract can be discharged by performance, agreement, frustration or by acceptance of a repudiatory breach. (See *Nutshell on Contract*.)

Where an agent earning commission, who is neither an employee not a self-employed commercial agent, is given authority for an indefinite period the principal can generally terminate the agency without giving notice. (*Levy v Goldhill* [1917].) If the agent is an employee then the express or implied terms of his contract, and possibly statutory provisions, will set the amount of notice which must be given. Where the agent is not an employee, but his contract is analogous to a contract of employment, then the agent is entitled to a reasonable period of notice. The length of the notice required is a matter of fact and will depend upon all the circumstances of the case. (*Martin Baker Aircraft Co Ltd v Canadian Flight Equipment Ltd* [1955].

If an agent is dismissed without being given the proper period of notice then the remedy will generally be damages rather than specific performance of the agency contract. As a general principle of contract law, specific performance of personal service contracts is not ordered. (*Warren v Mendy* 1989].)

Irrevocable agency

Some, very few, agencies are irrevocable. First, an agency coupled with an interest may be irrevocable. However, this cannot be the case unless the agency was created in return for some valuable consideration, and to protect an interest of the agent, which existed independently of the agency. Second, an agency might be irrevocable if there are implied terms of the contract that the agent should be indemnified for some personal liability which he has incurred, and also that the agency should not be revoked until he has been indemnified. Again, it must be stated that very few agencies are irrevocable. The principal can almost always withdraw the agent's actual authority at any time. This might be a breach of contract but the agent's actual authority will cease to exist.

Termination by operation of law

There are several ways in which agency might be terminated by the law. First, **the death of either the principal or the agent** will automatically terminate the agency. (Unless the agency was irrevocable.) This termination is, of course, only as regards the future. If a principal dies his personal representatives will take over his rights and obligations as regards contracts already created by the agent. In *Campanari v Woodburn* [1854] it was held that P's death automatically ended A's authority and it did not matter that A did not know that P was dead. Second, **the insanity of either the principal or agent** will automatically end any agency which was not irrevocable. Third, **the bankruptcy of the principal** will automatically end the agency. **The bankruptcy of the agent** will not terminate the agency unless it makes the agent unfit to further perform his duties.

Termination and apparent authority

The third party's position depends upon the way in which the agent's authority was terminated. If the principal withdrew the agent's actual authority then the agent might still have apparent authority, as long as T did not know that the agent's authority had been withdrawn. It seems likely that where the agent's authority is terminated on account of the principal having become incapacitated, then the agent's apparent authority should also be terminated. This seems to be the position where the principal has died or become bankrupt. Where the principal has become insane the position is less clear. In *Drew v Nunn* [1879] A's apparent authority was not terminated by P's insanity. In *Yonge v Toynbee* [1910] P became insane and A, who did not know this, was liable for breach of warranty of authority as regards contracts made after this time. This liability arose because P was not liable, the insanity having removed A's apparent authority. (Section 2 of the Enduring Power of Attorney Act 1985 now absolves an agent appointed under an enduring power of authority from liability in these circumstances, but it does not alter the principle of this case.)

TERMINATION UNDER THE COMMERCIAL AGENTS (COUNCIL DIRECTIVE) REGULATIONS 1993

The 1993 Regs can give agents a right to an indemnity or to compensation upon the termination of the agency. However, in order to qualify an agent must fit within the definition of a self-employed commercial agent.

The definition of a commercial agent

Regulation 2(1) defines a commercial agent to whom the Regs apply. First, it requires the agent to be "self-employed", although it seems that a company or partnership could qualify. Second, the agent must "negotiate and conclude" contracts for the sale or purchase of goods. If the principal sets the price then it may be the case that the agent will not be regarded as having negotiated the contract. Agents who negotiate and conclude the sale or purchase of services rather than goods will not be included. The agent must negotiate and conclude the contract "on behalf of" the principal. This would therefore exclude those people, such as motor dealers, who describe themselves as agents but are in fact not agents as they buy and sell on their own behalf. Third, the contract must also be negotiated and concluded 'in the name of the principal' and so an undisclosed agent cannot be within the Regs. Fourth, the agent's authority must be 'continuing' and so an agent employed to make only one contract cannot be included. Fifth, company officers, partners and insolvency practitioners are excluded from the definition. So are commercial agents when they operate on commodity exchanges or in the commodity market.

Finally, the commercial agency must not be "secondary". (Regulation 2(4).) The Schedule to the Regs gives guidance on deciding when activities are secondary. Paragraphs 1 and 2 of the Schedule say that the activities are to be secondary if: the principal's business is not the purchase or sale of goods of a particular kind; the goods are not such that transactions are normally individually negotiated and concluded on a commercial basis; and making a deal on one occasion is not likely to lead to more deals for the principal so that it would be in the commercial interest of the principal to appoint an agent to develop that market. Paragraph 3 lists matters which indicate that an agent is a commercial agent. These are: that the principal is the manufacturer, importer or distributor of the goods; that the goods are specifically identified with the principal; that the agent devotes substantially the whole of his time on his agency activities (even if for more than one principal); that the goods are not normally available in the market except through the agent; and that the agent is described as a commercial agent.

Paragraph 4 says that if promotional material is supplied direct to customers, or if customers normally select the goods themselves and merely place their orders through an agent, then these are indications that there is no commercial agency. Mail order catalogue agents for consumer goods and consumer credit agents are specifically excluded by para.5.

Rights of the commercial agent on termination of the contract

Notice

Commercial agents are given minimum periods of notice. These periods of notice must conclude on the last day of the month. Longer periods can be agreed but shorter periods cannot. The notice can be given by either party, but the agent cannot be required to give more notice than the principal. Regulation 15 provides that where there is no fixed period of notice the minimum period is one month during the first year of the agency, two months during the second year and three months during the third or subsequent years. If a fixed period commercial agency ends and the agent continues to work for the principal then it is converted into an agency for an indefinite period by Reg.14 and the notice rules then apply. When assessing the period of notice the time worked under the fixed term agreement is taken into account.

Compensation

Regulation 17 entitles a commercial agent to compensation if the agency is terminated. This is the case whether the termination by the principal is wrongful or not. The compensation is to cover damage suffered by the agent. Regulation 17(7) deems that damage has been suffered in two situations. First, where the termination deprives the agent of the commission which the proper performance of the contract would have enabled him to make while the principal derives substantial benefit from the agent's activities. Second, where the agent has not been able to recoup the costs and expenses of performing the agency.

Indemnity

Unless the agency agreement provides otherwise, a commercial agent is entitled to be compensated rather than indemnified. If an indemnity is agreed, two conditions need to be fulfilled. First, the agent must have brought the principal new customers or have significantly increased the volume of business with existing customers and the principal must continue to derive substantial benefits from the business with such customers. Second, the payment of the indemnity must be equitable having regard to all the circumstances and, in particular, the commission lost by the commercial agent on the business transacted with such customers. The amount of the indemnity cannot exceed one year's commission, calculated by reference to the average commission of the agent over the previous five years. If the agent has not worked for five years it is the average commission over the period he has worked.

Loss of compensation and indemnity

Regulation 18 provides that no compensation or indemnity is payable in three circumstances. First, where the agent has committed a repudiatory breach which justified his dismissal. Second, where the agent terminates the contract. (Unless this is in acceptance of the principal's repudiatory breach or made necessary by age, illness or infirmity.) Third, where the agent has assigned his rights and liabilities to a third party.

11. EXAMINATION CHECKLIST

Definitions

Can you define:

    (a) a contract of sale of goods;
    (b) a sale;
    (c) an agreement to sell;
    (d) specific goods;
    (e) unascertained goods;
    (f) existing goods; and
    (g) future goods?

The statutory implied terms

1. Have you classified the contract as one of sale of goods, or of hire-purchase, or for the transfer of property in goods or of hire?
2. Remember that the terms as to the right to sell, correspondence with description and correspondence with sample are implied whether or not the sale was made in the course of a business.
3. Have you remembered that if the term as to the right to sell is breached then the buyer can reclaim all of the price even if the goods have been used or consumed?
4. Have you remembered that s.15A SGA 1979 prevents a buyer who does not deal as a consumer from rejecting if the breach of ss.13, 14(2), 14(3) or 15 is so slight that it would be unreasonable to reject?
5. Remember that the terms as to satisfactory quality and fitness for purpose are implied only if the seller sells in the course of a business and that *Stevenson v Rogers* gives the meaning of this.
6. Check that you know the two circumstances in which s.14(2C) SGA will act as a defence to a claim under s.14(2).
7. Remember to apply the definition of satisfactory quality (in SGA s.14(2A)) before applying the aspects of quality in appropriate cases (in s.14(2B)).
8. Are you sure that you know the requirements of the term as to fitness for purpose and the circumstances in which the term will not be implied?

9. Can you explain the two terms implied into a sale by sample?
10. What is the UCTA s.12(1) definition of dealing as a consumer? Is this definition also used by the SGA 1979?
11. Can you outline the extent to which UCTA 1977 allows the statutory implied terms to be excluded?
12. Can you describe the circumstances in which the 1999 UTCC Regulations may render a term of a contract ineffective?

The transfer of property

1. Are you sure that you have correctly classified the goods as being specific or unascertained at the time of the contract?
2. If the goods are specific, have you considered s.17? If s.17 does not apply, have you decided which Rule of s.18 to apply? Can you apply the test to decide whether goods are in a deliverable state?
3. If the goods are unascertained, are you sure you have got past s.16? Have you then considered s.17? Can you apply the test to decide whether the goods have been unconditionally appropriated to the contract? Can you list all the requirements of appropriation by exhaustion?
4. Can you list all the requirements necessary for a buyer to become a co-owner of unascertained goods forming part of a bulk? Can you calculate the extent of the buyer's co-ownership?
5. Can you explain the meaning of the risk and the rules on risk while the goods are in transit?
6. Do you know the rules on mistake and frustration? Do you know the meaning of perishing?
7. Which sections of the SGA allow for retention of title clauses? Have you checked that the ROT clause has been incorporated into the contract?
8. Are you familiar with the different types of ROT clauses? Can you explain the arguments as to why certain types of ROT clauses might be void as unregistered charges?

Sale by a person who is not the owner

1. Can you explain the principle *nemo dat quod non habet*?
2. Can you list all the requirements necessary for a mercantile agent to pass a good title?

3. Can you explain the circumstances in which estoppel will defeat the *nemo dat* principle?
4. Can you explain the circumstances in which a person with only a voidable title to goods can nevertheless pass a good title? If this exception does not help a person who bought from a rogue who acquired goods with a bad cheque, have you remembered to consider the buyer in possession exception?
5. How does the seller in possession exception to the *nemo dat quod non habet* principle work? Can you list all the requirements?
6. How does the buyer in possession exception to the *nemo dat quod non habet* principle work? Can you list all the requirements?
7. In what circumstances can a person who has taken a motor vehicle on HP pass a good title before himself acquiring a good title under the HP agreement?
8. Can a person who has stolen goods ever pass title to those goods?

Duties of the buyer and the seller

1. Can you explain the meaning of delivery, and the SGA rules about the time and place of delivery?
2. Can you explain the legal position if the wrong quantity of goods is delivered?
3. Can you explain the circumstances in which a buyer can terminate the whole contract on account of one instalment being defective?
4. Do you know the rules about delivery to a carrier?
5. How might the price of the goods be fixed?
6. What is the difference between the buyer's duty to accept and the duty to take delivery?
7. Can you define an unpaid seller?
8. Can you describe the rights available to an unpaid seller against the goods, and the circumstances in which each right is available?

Remedies of the parties

1. In what circumstances can the seller sue for the price?
2. Can you explain how damages for non-acceptance are assessed? Do you know how the market rule operates?

3. Can you explain how damages for refusal to take delivery are assessed?
4. Can you explain the circumstances in which a seller is entitled to treat the contract as terminated?
5. Can you explain how damages for non-delivery are assessed? Do you know how the market rule operates?
6. Can you explain how damages for breach of warranty are assessed?
7. Can you explain the circumstances in which a buyer is entitled to reject the goods?
8. Do you know the significance of the buyer accepting the goods, and the ways in which a buyer is deemed to have accepted?
9. Can you explain the buyer's right of partial rejection?
10. Do you know the circumstances in which additional rights are available to buyers in consumer cases?
11. Can you describe the first and second tier rights available to buyers in consumer cases, and the circumstances in which the second tier rights become available?

International sales

1. Do you know what a bill of lading is?
2. Can you describe the legal effect of a bill of lading as evidence of the contract of carriage, as a receipt and as a document of title?
3. Can you explain the duties of the parties to an FOB contract?
4. When do the property and the risk pass in an FOB contract?
5. Can you explain the duties of the parties to a CIF contract?
5. When do the property and the risk pass in a CIF contract?

Agency

1. Can you explain how actual authority arises and the difference between express actual authority and implied actual authority?
2. Can you explain how apparent authority arises?
3. Can you explain the consequences of an agent having actual authority?
4. What are the requirements of ratification? What is the effect of ratification?

5. Can you explain the consequences of an agent having apparent but not actual authority?
6. Can you explain the decision in *Watteau v Fenwick*?
7. Can you describe the different ways in which an agent might be said to have "usual authority"?
8. How can agency arise by operation of law?
9. Can you distinguish disclosed and undisclosed agency?
10. Can you explain the doctrine of the undisclosed principal, and the circumstances in which an undisclosed principal cannot intervene on the contract?
11. Can you explain the different ways in which a third party might gain rights against the agent?
12. Can you explain the duties which an agent owes to his principal?
13. Can you explain the rights which an agent might have against his principal?
14. How might an agent's authority be terminated?
15. In what circumstances might an agency be irrevocable?
16. Can you outline the definition of a self-employed commercial agent, and the rights of such an agent to an indemnity or compensation?

12. SAMPLE EXAMINATION QUESTIONS AND MODEL ANSWERS

Question 1

Six months ago Bill, a market gardener, bought a new tractor from a dealer. The police have now taken the tractor from Bill and returned to its true owner, Jo. A thief had stolen the tractor from Jo, before selling it to the dealer. The dealer did not know that the tractor had been stolen.

Two months ago Bill bought a ton of fertiliser and a second-hand rotovator from Sid, a dealer in agricultural goods, whose business is nearby. Sid described the fertiliser as organic two year old fertiliser. In fact it was organic 18 month old fertiliser. The fact that the fertiliser was only 18 months old, rather than two years old, did not affect its quality. Bill has now been offered a very cheap ton of fertiliser by someone else and would now like to reject the fertiliser delivered by Sid. Bill is claiming that he never uses fertiliser which is less than two years old, a matter of which Sid was unaware, and that his own advertising stresses this.

Before Bill bought the rotovator Sid pointed out that one of its blades was cracked. He also said that it was three years old and that over the years it had had a good deal of heavy use. Bill is now rejecting the rotovator on the following grounds. First, the cracked blade makes the rotovator unsuitable for use on his soil, which is very heavy. Second, the bodywork of the rotovator is badly dented. Third, the rotovator's petrol tank had a slight leak and will need to be replaced.

Advise Bill of his legal position. To what extent could an exclusion clause restrict or exclude any liability which might arise?

Answer 1

As the dealer did not own the tractor when he sold it to Bill he would not have had the right to sell it and would therefore have breached s.12(1) SGA 1979. It will be immaterial that the dealer acted innocently. Applying *Rowland v Divall*, Bill will not be deemed to have accepted the goods and can therefore reject them despite having used them for six months. Furthermore, Bill can reclaim the whole of the purchase price as there will have been a total failure of consideration on the dealer's part.

The quality of the fertiliser is not affected by its misdescription and so s.14(2) will not be applicable. However, s.13(1) might have been breached. A number of questions will need to be answered to see if this is the case. Was the description of the goods, as two years old, a term of the contract? As the goods were unascertained goods, it seems likely that the parties did intend the description to be a term. On the assumption that it was a term, we then need to ask what type of term it was. If the term is not within s.13 then it is likely to be an innominate term and, as the breach will not have deprived Bill of substantially the whole benefit of the contract, termination of the contract will not be possible. Furthermore, only nominal damages would be available as the breach has caused no real loss. Bill will therefore want to argue that the term was within s.13(1), as the term implied by s.13(1) is a condition. Was the description a description by which the goods were sold? As the goods were unascertained goods, and as they were sold in a commercial context, Bill might be able to establish that they were sold by reference to the description. Next Bill would need to establish that the description identified the type of goods which were being sold. He would need to show that the description identified a substantial ingredient of the identity of the goods.

Section 13 is a condition and so if it were breached Bill would initially have the right to reject the goods. However, he could not reject the goods if he has accepted them. (Section 11(4).) As Bill has retained the goods for five weeks without rejecting them, he would probably be deemed to have accepted them under s.35(4). Bill will therefore be able to claim damages for breach of warranty but will not be able to terminate the contract. Furthermore, it seems likely that Bill did not deal as a consumer, despite the decision in *R & B Customs Brokers v United Dominions Trust Ltd*, because he had bought this type of fertiliser for his business fairly regularly. Therefore, if the breach of s.13 was so slight that it would be unreasonable to reject then s.15A would also compel Bill to treat the breach of condition as a breach of warranty. As the breach was not of a warranty of quality, damages would be assessed under s.53(2). The measure of damages might be the cost of buying replacement fertiliser which matched the contract description, less the amount which Bill could get for the fertiliser supplied to him.

As regards the rotovator, Bill might have a claim under s.14(2) or 14(3). The rotovator was sold in the course of a business as it was sold by a business. (*Stevenson v Rogers*.) First, it is clear that the cracked blade cannot make the goods unsatisfactory as this defect was specifically pointed out to Bill before the contract was made. (Section 14(2C)(a).) As regards the bodywork, the examination which Bill conducted would seem to operate as a defence under s.14(2C)(b). Even a cursory examination ought to have revealed this defect. The leak in the petrol tank might mean that the goods were not of satisfactory quality. This would be the case if the presence of the leak would have caused the reasonable person to regard the goods as unsatisfactory, taking account of the price, the description and all of the relevant circumstances. The age of the goods, and the fact that it was pointed out that they had had a good deal of use might suggest otherwise, but it seems likely that the reasonable person would not regard the goods of satisfactory quality when sold. The leak in the petrol tank is more than a minor defect, and might possibly make the goods unsafe, and so it might be thought that s.14(2B) would automatically mean that the goods were not of satisfactory quality. However, the five matters set out in s.14(2B) are only aspects of quality in appropriate cases. Bearing in mind the age of the rotovator, and the description of it, this does not seem an appropriate case to require freedom from minor defects. It might be an appropriate case to regard safety as an aspect of the rotovator's quality, and if so this might strengthen the view that the reasonable person would not regard the rotovator as satisfactory.

Section 14(3) would not have been breached unless Bill made his particular purpose known to the seller. This could be done impliedly and so it would be enough that the seller knew that Bill's soil was very heavy. But even if that were the case, the fact that the seller pointed out the cracked blade would seem to indicate that there was no reliance on the seller's skill and judgement.

Two months seems longer than a reasonable time to examine the goods to see whether they conform to the contract, and so it seems likely that Bill will be deemed by s.35(4) to have accepted the goods. Therefore, he will be unable to reject them. He will be able to claim damages for breach of warranty under s.53. The damages will be assessed under s.53(3) as the warranty was one of quality and will prima facie be the difference between the value the rotovator actually had and the value it would have had if there had been no breach of s.14(2).

If we assume that exclusion clauses had been incorporated into the contracts, and that they covered the breaches which occurred, it then becomes necessary to consider the Unfair Contract Terms Act 1977. First, the breach of s.12(1) SGA cannot be excluded or restricted by any contract term, and so an exclusion clause could not restrict or exclude the liability of the dealer who sold the tractor

In order to decide whether liability for the breaches of ss.13(1) and 14(2) could be excluded we would first need to see whether Bill dealt as a consumer when he made the contracts in question. Section 61(5A) SGA directs us to s.12(1) UCTA, which sets out two requirements which need to be fulfilled. First, Bill needs to have made the contracts otherwise than in the course of a business. Second, Sid needs to have made the contracts in the course of a business. Sid did make both contracts in the course of a business as the goods he sold were the type of goods he was in business to sell. As regards the fertiliser, Bill will have made the contract in the course of a business because he has bought fertiliser on behalf of the business with a sufficient degree of regularity. Bill will therefore not have dealt as a consumer and so UCTA will allow liability for breach of s.13 to be excluded to the extent that this satisfies the UCTA require-ment of reasonableness. The indicative factors set out in Sch.2 would have to be considered. It would seem that Bill could have bought alternative goods from a different supplier without agreeing to a similar exclusion clause and so it is likely that the exclusion clause would satisfy the requirement of reasonable-ness and could validly exclude or restrict liability for the breach.

As regards the rotovator, Bill might well have dealt as a consumer. Applying *R & B Customs Brokers*, the fact that he bought the goods for business use will not necessarily mean that he did not deal as a consumer. If this was the first rotovator which he had bought then Bill will have dealt as a consumer. If he did deal as a consumer, s.6 UCTA would prevent the exclusion or restriction of liability for the breach of s.14(2). If Bill had bought other rotovators, with such a degree of regularity that the purchase could be regarded as an integral part of his business, then he will not have dealt as a consumer. Then s.6 UCTA would allow liability for the breach of s.14(2) to be excluded or restricted to the extent that this satisfied the UCTA requirement of reasonableness.

The UTCC Regulations 1999 would not be applicable because, under those Regs, Bill was not a consumer. In the Regs a consumer is defined as a natural person who is acting for purposes outside his trade, business or profession. (Reg.3(1).)

Question 2

Ace Ltd manufactures only one type of radio. Last week Ace received orders for radios from three separate customers. Bert ordered 50 radios, Chas ordered 10 and David ordered 90. Bert and Chas both paid the full price but David paid nothing. Ace Ltd agreed to send the radios to the three customers.

Ace Ltd put 50 radios in a crate addressed to Bert and 100 radios in a second crate. A driver from Edwina's Carriers arrived to collect the radios. The driver was told to deliver the crate of 50 radios to Bert. The driver was also told to deliver 10 of the radios from the second crate to Chas and the remaining 90 to David.

The driver first delivered 10 radios to Chas, as instructed. However, the lorry was then involved in an accident and all of the radios remaining on the lorry (those destined for both Bert and David) were damaged. The accident was caused by an unidentified motorist.

Advise the parties of their legal positions. How would your advice differ if David had telephoned Ace Ltd immediately after the lorry driver had arrived at Ace Ltd's premises and had been told that his 90 radios were part of a consignment of 100 radios on board the lorry which had just departed?

Answer 2

Chas

There is no problem re Chas. He has paid for and received his 10 radios.

Did Bert have the risk at the time of the accident?

Under s.20(1) risk will pass at the same time as the property, as the parties have not agreed otherwise. The radios which Bert contracted to buy are unascertained goods, because the actual radios sold were not identified and agreed upon at the time of the contract, and so were not specific goods as defined by s.61(1). Section 20A is not applicable as no bulk was identified. The goods were ascertained when put into the crate and labelled with Bert's name, so s.16 has been satisfied. (As per Atkin L.J. in *Re Wait*). Section 17 seems inapplicable as the parties did not show any intention as to when property should pass. The property and the risk would have passed when the goods were delivered to the carrier. (Sections 18 Rule 5(2), 20(1) and 32(1).) The damage to the goods happened after this and so Bert will have no remedy against Ace Ltd.

Did David have the risk at the time of the accident?

The risk will pass at the same time as the property as the parties have not agreed otherwise. (Section 20(1).) David contracted to buy unascertained goods. Section 20A is not applicable as no part of the price was paid, and also because no bulk was identified. The goods were not ascertained when put on the lorry. So s.18 Rule 5(2) would not have passed the property and s.32(1) would not have passed the risk. Even when 10 radios were delivered to Chas, there might have been ascertainment but there was no unconditional appropriation to which David had assented and so property and risk would not have passed to him. The bulk was never identified by the parties to the contract, and so property will not pass under s.18 Rule 5(2). David will not have to pay for the radios and will have a claim for damages unless 90 other radios which match the contract description are delivered to him.

What if David had been told that his radios were to come from the unsealed crate of 100 radios?

The risk will pass at the same time as the property as the parties have not agreed otherwise. (Section 20(1).) David contracted to buy unascertained goods. Section 20A is not applicable as no part of the price was paid. When the 10 radios were delivered to Chas, David's goods would have become ascertained and appropriated by exhaustion. Property in the remaining 90 radios would have passed to David under s.18 Rule 5(3). All of the requirements of s.18 Rule5(3) would be satisfied. First, there was a sale of a specified quantity of unascertained goods forming part of a bulk. Second, this bulk was identified after the contract, by subsequent agreement between the parties. Third, the bulk was reduced to the amount of goods due to the buyer. Finally, the buyer was the only buyer to whom goods were then due out of the bulk. As property had passed risk would also have passed. (Section 20(1).) Therefore, the radios were at David's risk when damaged and he will have to pay the price of them.

Question 3

Mark took a car on hire-purchase from New Finance Ltd, who owned the car. The agreement was to run for three years, but after paying only two monthly instalments Mark sold the car to Oliver. Oliver works as a mechanic for a local garage but buys and sells cars for profit in his spare time. Oliver subjected the car to an HPI check but this did not reveal that the car was the subject of a hire-purchase agreement because New Finance Ltd had neglected to register the car with HPI.

Oliver sold the car to Peter, a teacher, for £5,000. Peter did not know that the car was subject to the hire-purchase agreement. Peter soon found that the car was not roomy enough for him and that driving it gave him backache. Peter left the car with Quentin's garage, asking Quentin to service the car and sell it at a price of not less than £4,500. Quentin's garage generally services cars rather than sells them, but does occasionally sell cars on behalf of established customers.

Roger saw the car at Quentin's garage and bought it for £4,000. Quentin took a cheque from Roger and allowed him to drive the car away. Roger was rather absent minded and had forgotten that his bank account had insufficient funds to make the purchase. This caused his cheque to be dishonoured. Quentin informed Peter that the cheque has been dishonoured and Peter contacted the police and the major motoring organisations, asking them to look out for the car. Later Roger advertised sold the car to Steve, whom he had met in the pub. New Finance Ltd have now contacted Steve to demand that the car is returned to them.

Advise the parties of their rights and obligations.

Answer 3

Mark never became the owner of the car because he did not complete his payments under the hire-purchase contract. He had neither bought nor agreed to buy the car and so could not pass title as a buyer in possession. (*Helby v Mathews*).

Oliver might argue that, by failing to register the car with HPI, New Finance Ltd had made a representation that the car was not the subject of a hire-purchase agreement, and that they would be estopped from denying this later. However in *Moorgate Mercantile v Twitchings* the House of Lords rejected such an argument by a bare majority of 3:2. Oliver is not a private purchase for purposes of HPA 1964 and so does not become owner of the car by virtue of that Act. (*Stevenson v Beverley Bentinck Ltd*). Oliver can sue Mark for damages under s.12(1).

There is nothing in the question to indicate that Peter is not acting in good faith. Therefore as the first private purchaser of the car, and assuming that he was acting in good faith, Peter acquired title to the car under HPA 1964 Part III. The title which Peter will acquire is the title which New Finance Ltd had, that is to say, complete ownership. New Finance Ltd, having lost title to the car, can sue Mark on the hire-purchase agreement.

Quentin had no actual authority to sell the car to Roger for £4000, as he was told to get at least £4,500 for it. (*Waugh v Clifford*). Nor would Peter's leaving the car with Quentin give Quentin apparent authority to sell the car. Quentin would seem to fulfil the requirements of s.2(1) Factors Act 1889 and might therefore pass title as a mercantile agent. First, Quentin must buy or sell goods on behalf of others in a business capacity, which he does. Second, when he sold the goods on to Roger he possessed the goods. Third, he gained possession with the owner's consent. Fourth, possession of the goods was given to Quentin for a purpose connected with sale. Fifth, he sold the goods in the ordinary course of business of a mercantile agent, in business hours, from business premises and in other ways acting as the third party would expect a mercantile agent to be acting. Finally, Roger must take the goods in good faith and without knowing that the mercantile agent had no authority to sell them. The burden of proof is on Roger. (*Heap v Motorist's Advisory Agency Ltd* [1923].) Section 61(3) SGA makes it plain that the test of good faith is a subjective one and so Roger will not fail to gain title merely because his cheque was dishonoured.

However, as Roger made an actionable misrepresentation, the title which he would have gained would not be complete title, but a voidable title. The misrepresentation would be negligent, as Roger was careless rather than dishonest. In *Car and Universal Finance Ltd v Caldwell* the Court of Appeal left open the question whether or not a contract induced by a negligent misrepresenta-tion could be avoided otherwise than by informing the mis-representor. If the contract had not been avoided then Steve would have gained a good title to the car, under s.23, provided that he bought it in good faith and without notice. It would be up to Peter to show that Roger did not act in good faith. Peter could sue Quentin for damages for his failure to obey his instructions as an agent.

If the contract was avoided then s.23 will not apply. However, Steve could still argue that title passed to him by virtue of s.25. On the face of it, s.25 would seem to apply. However, the restrictive interpretation given in *Newtons of Wembley v Williams* would have to be considered. In that case the Court of Appeal interpreted the final words of s.25 literally, to say that title would not be passed unless the buyer in possession happened to sell the car in the same way in which he would be required to sell it to be within s.2(1) Factors Act. That is to say, only if he sold it in the ordinary course of business of a mercantile agent. Roger does not seem to have sold the car in this way and so Steve would not gain title under s.25. Peter could reclaim the car from Steve. Steve could sue Roger for damages for breach of s.12(1).

Question 4

Alan runs and owns a small garage. When Alan booked his three week annual holiday he arranged that his foreman, Billy, would run the garage while he was away. Billy was told that he could sell any car on the forecourt, as long as he got at least 90 per cent of the price displayed on the car. He was told not to buy any cars at all, no matter what the circumstances.

While Alan was away Billy sold a car to Carol for 85 per cent of the price shown on the car. Carol thought that Billy owned the business.

Dinah, who regularly did business with Alan, bought a car for 75 per cent of the price shown on it. She knew that Alan usually insisted on at least 90 per cent of the price shown, even when the buyer was, as she was, in the motor trade. She asked Billy whether he was sure he could sell the car at 75 per cent of the price shown. Billy, untruthfully, said that Alan had told him to do this if the buyer was a motor dealer. Dinah therefore bought the car and paid for it.

Billy bought a car from Elizabeth because he was sure that it was such a bargain that Alan would want it. Alan examined the car when he returned from his holiday and considered it a good buy. Elizabeth has now discovered that the car was worth more than she thought. Hearing from Billy that he should not really have sold the car, Elizabeth intends to reclaim the car. However, Alan has telephoned her to say that she will not be able to claim the return of the car as he has definitely bought it. Elizabeth refuses to accept that she cannot reclaim the car.

Alan does not want to be bound by the contracts which Billy made with Carol and Dinah. Nor is he willing to let Elizabeth reclaim the car which she sold. Advise Alan of his legal position in respect of the above facts.

Answer 4

Carol

Billy had no actual or apparent authority to make the contract. Actual authority, whether express or implied, arises by agreement between principal and agent. (*Hely-Hutchinson v Brayhead Ltd.*) Billy plainly did not have express actual authority to sell a car for 85 per cent of its displayed price as he was told that he could sell cars only if he got at least 90 per cent of the displayed price. Nor would he have had implied actual authority. The principal, Alan, expressly prohibited Billy from acting as he did, and so it is not possible to argue that Alan impliedly agreed that Billy should act in this way. (*Waugh v Clifford.*) Carol will not be able to claim that Billy had apparent authority. Such authority could arise only if Alan had made a representation to Carol that Billy had authority to sell the car. But this cannot have happened if Carol thought that Billy owned the business. Billy would seem to have 'usual authority' of the type which arose in *Watteau v Fenwick*. Although this case has been criticised, and although it has not been followed in some Commonwealth courts, it would still appear to be a binding precedent. If it were followed, Alan would be bound by the contract but could claim against Billy for failure to obey instructions. If it were not followed, Alan would not be bound by the contract but Billy would be personally liable on the contract.

Dinah

As already explained in relation to the car sold to Carol, Billy had no actual authority to make the sale as in doing so he contravened his express instructions. (*Waugh v Clifford*). Generally, a principal who appoints an agent to a certain position will be taken to have represented to outsiders who deal with the agent that the agent had authority to make such contracts as an agent occupying such a position would usually make. Consequently the agent would have apparent authority to make such contracts and they would be binding on the principal. (*Hely-Hutchinson v Brayhead Ltd.*) Here though there would there be apparent authority, as Dinah knows that Billy has no actual authority. (*Armagas.*) Billy cannot himself make the representation to Dinah that he has authority. Therefore there would have been no apparent authority and Alan will not be bound by the contract. Billy might be liable to Dinah for breach of warranty of authority. Damages for such a breach would be assessed under *Hadley v Baxendale*. Dinah would therefore be compensated for loss of the bargain which she had made. However this would not be the case if Dinah actually knew that Billy had no authority.

Elizabeth

Alan had no actual authority to make the purchase. He might well have had apparent authority to do so but this would not allow Alan to enforce the contract. (It would allow Elizabeth to enforce it against Alan, but she does not want to do this.) However, as long as Billy made the contract in Alan's name, Alan has effectively ratified the contract. The effect of this would be that Billy would have had actual authority, retrospectively from the time when he made the contract, and so Elizabeth would be bound by the contract and Billy would have no liability. (*Bolton Partners v Lambert*.) If Billy did not make the contract in Alan's name then there would be no effective ratification and Elizabeth would not be bound by the contract.

INDEX

LEGAL TAXONOMY

FROM SWEET & MAXWELL

This index has been prepared using Sweet and Maxwell's Legal Taxonomy. Main index entries conform to keywords provided by the Legal Taxonomy except where references to specific documents or non-standard terms (denoted by quotation marks) have been included. These keywords provide a means of identifying similar concepts in other Sweet & Maxwell publications and online services to which keywords from the Legal Taxonomy have been applied. Readers may find some minor differences between terms used in the text and those which appear in the index. Suggestions to *taxonomy@sweetandmaxwell.co.uk*.

(all references are to page number)